BAIL
ME OUT!

Gerald W. Bracey

BAIL ME OUT!

**Handling Difficult Data and Tough Questions
About Public Schools**

CORWIN PRESS, INC.
A Sage Publications Company
Thousand Oaks, California

For information:

Corwin Press, Inc.
A Sage Publications Company
2455 Teller Road
Thousand Oaks, California 91320
E-mail: order@corwinpress.com

Sage Publications Ltd.
6 Bonhill Street
London EC2A 4PU
United Kingdom

Sage Publications India Pvt. Ltd.
M-32 Market
Greater Kailash I
New Delhi 110 048 India

Printed in the United States of America

Library of Congress Cataloging-in-Publication Data

Bracey, Gerald W. (Gerald Watking)
   Bail me out!: Handling difficult data and tough questions about
public schools / by Gerald W. Bracey.
       p. cm.
Includes bibliographical references.
   ISBN 0-7619-7602-7 (cloth: acid-free paper)
   ISBN 0-7619-7603-5 (pbk.: acid-free paper)
   1. Public schools—United States. 2. Teachers—United States.
I. Title.
LA217.2.B72 2000
371.01'0973—dc21   99-050787

This book is printed on acid-free paper.

00 01 02 03 04 05 10 9 8 7 6 5 4 3 2 1

Corwin Editorial Assistant: Kylee Leigl
Production Editor: Denise Santoyo
Editorial Assistant: Victoria Cheng
Typesetter/Designer: Danielle Dillahunt
Cover Designer: Tracy E. Miller

Contents

About the Author

Gerald W. Bracey, a nationally known policy analyst, researcher, and author, loves to separate public education myth from reality in his lectures and writings. Bracey, a Virginia native, well known for his monthly educational research columns in *Phi Delta Kappan* and his periodic "Bracey Report on the Condition of Public Education," has drawn the attention of national media. His article, "Why Can't They Be Like We Were?" now known as "The First Bracey Report," drew the wrath of the Bush administration for his refutation of statements made in *A Nation at Risk*, a national education report commissioned by President Bush.

Bracey has been a research psychologist for the Educational Testing Service, associate director of the Institute for Child Study at Indiana University-Bloomington, and has served for 9 years as the director of research, evaluation, and testing for the Virginia Department of Education. He is the author of several recent publications, including *Put to the Test: An Educator's and Consumer's Guide to Standardized Testing; Setting the Record Straight: Responses to Misconceptions About Public Education in the United States* (1997); *The TRUTH About America's Public Schools: The Bracey Reports, 1991-1997* (1997); and *Understanding Education Statistics: It's Easier (And More Important) Than You Think* (1997).

Introduction

Why You Need a Book Like This

You need a book like this for four reasons: (a) You need to be able to READ the data. (b) You need to read the DATA. (c) You need to be able to discuss the concept of "achievement" in all of its ramifications, not just in terms of test scores. (d) You need some perspective on how we got to the place we are in the first place. Let's talk about these reasons for a moment. Consider the following quote:

> Nationally, teachers—public and private—are 50% more likely than the public at large to choose private schools (17.1% to 13.1%). Not too make too fine a point, teachers, public and private, white and black, Hispanic and non-Hispanic, low income, middle income, and high income, know how to address the nation's education crisis: they vote with their feet and their pocketbooks. . . . If private schools are good enough for public school teachers, why aren't they good enough for poor children? . . . With teachers choosing private schools, the truth is self-evident: while they work in public schools they choose private schools for their own children because they believe they are better. They are connoisseurs. And no one in our society is better qualified to make that judgment than teachers. (Doyle, 1994, p. 3)

Doyle penned his passage in an ominous tone. He implies that public school teachers of all stripes are a treacherous bunch, abandoning their own institutions in favor of private schools. Teachers are connoisseurs. One definition of connoisseur is "a person with informed and discriminating taste." Teachers, therefore, know what good schools look like and send their kids to them. They send their kids to private schools. Certainly, this is the impression left by the rhetoric. It is what you would come away with if you did not actually look at Doyle's results.

When we actually read the data, Doyle's rhetoric fades fast. First off, Doyle claims that teachers are 50% more likely to choose private schools than the general public—17.1% to 13.1%. This is an arithmetical error. The larger figure is only 30% larger than the smaller one. Did Doyle commit this mistake on purpose, figuring that no one would notice? Given his ideology, it could be. In any case, his 50% claim is wrong.

Second, the 17.1% figure contains both public and private school teachers, not just public school teachers, something Doyle mentions only briefly. He clearly implies that it is *public* school teachers who refuse to let their kids attend the institutions they work in: "If private schools are good enough for public school teachers, why aren't they good enough for poor children?" Ignoring that this is a non sequitur, we can still determine that the contention is false from Doyle's data. In one sentence, Doyle is forced to acknowledge that public school teachers *don't* use private schools a great deal: "Yet public school teachers as a group choose private schools less often than the public at large, by a one-point margin, 12.1% to 13.1%." How it must have pained Doyle to write that sentence. It is quickly sloughed over in favor of the portentous rhetoric that pervades the monograph.

So, you actually have to READ the data, not just the rhetoric, to know what is going on. And you have to be able to read the DATA to properly interpret its meaning. There's an arithmetical error to deal with. The figure that Doyle cites as implicating public school teachers actually includes private school teachers.

But there is more. What kinds of families are prone to use private schools? Wealthier and better educated families are more likely to buy into the notion that private schools are superior. This *should* lead more teachers to use private schools. While some 25% of all adults 25 and older have at least a bachelor's degree, virtually 100% of teachers do. In fact, the proportion of teachers owning at least a *master's* degree is *double* the proportion of the public who hold a bachelor's, more than 50%.

In addition, while teachers do not receive princely sums for their endeavors, they are usually not the only wage earners in the household, either. The year of Doyle's study, 1994, teachers' commanded about $35,000 for their services, but their household incomes were double that. In spite of their educational levels and wealth, teachers still stick with public schools more than the public at large.

Actually, the report shows that private school teachers are more inclined to use public schools than private schools. Doyle's data reveal that only 32.7% of private school teachers send their kids to private schools.

Difficulties in interpretation can occur in texts that carry smaller loads of partisan rhetoric. Data are not really data. *Data* is Latin for "givens" and nothing in the world of educational statistics is "given." It is constructed and must be interpreted. For example, while NAEP (National Assessment of Educational Progress) scores have been rising somewhat over the past decade, for many years most of the trendlines were relatively flat. Some people called the flatness "stagnation." Others called it "stability," arguing that there was no reason to expect NAEP, an assessment system not linked to any curriculum, to rise. Indeed, Archie Lapointe, the former executive director of NAEP, commented that the principal problem with NAEP was keeping kids awake for the tests. Since the test entered and left the students' lives on the same day and never returned with any impact on the student, the teacher, the principal, the superintendent, or the parents, it was hard to get kids motivated. Anecdotally, when a district I worked in participated in a try-out for NAEP state-by-state comparisons, about half of the teachers reported to me that they had trouble keeping the kids (eighth graders) on task.

People wonder about the recent increases in NAEP scores. These can be interpreted as reflecting the fact that more and more students are taking more and more academic courses in high school. There is probably something to this. On the other hand, in the most recent NAEP reading assessment, those states with the biggest gains since the previous testing are states with the biggest increases in the number of students excluded from testing.

Thus, it is important to READ the data and to read the DATA. Part I of this book attempts to make you a better, wiser reader.

The ability of public schools to attract the children of the teachers is not usually thought of as a measure of "achievement." But, in the broadest sense, it is. Part II of this book will elaborate on dimensions of achievement that mostly are not test related, but that are important nonetheless. In fact, with the current madness for test scores only, it is all the more important to hang onto and remember broad considerations of achievement.

Finally, it is important to know what is going on. Recently, while conducting a series of workshops for the Institute for the Development of Educational Activities (IDEA), over lunch someone referred to me as a "numbers guy." It's true, but today everyone needs to be a numbers guy. It used to be that the only data of concern to teachers and administrators were those concerning budgets and personnel. No more. School people who do not know what the data actually say about schools are vulnerable not only to half-truths and spun data, but to the perseveration of myths about schools. Some of these myths are remarkably long lived in spite of data refuting them.

For instance, Doyle's study that shows 12.1% of public school teachers send their children to private schools appeared in early 1995. Still, the editorial of July 7, 1998, in the *Florida Times Union* began this way: "Here's a Jeopardy-type puzzle: the president, vice president, half the U.S. Senate, a third of the House, and about 40% of public school teachers. The question is, who sends their children to private schools?" ("Allowing Choice," 1998).

Obviously, *Times Union* editors hadn't even read Doyle's rhetoric, much less his data. It is a wonderful aspect of journalism that editors don't have to provide citations for their sources. We can guess, though, that the source of the statements is two 1993 columns by *Washington Post* pundit George Will. In March 1993, Will noted that 43% of public school teachers in Chicago sent their children to private schools (Will, 1993a). In September of that same year, Will conveniently generalized this figure to the nation: "Nationally about half of urban school teachers with school age children send their children to private schools" (Will, 1993b). It is this sentence around which the *Times Union* editors apparently framed their quiz question.

On reading the column, I called Will's office for a citation. Will referred me to Clint Bolick of the Institute for Justice. Bolick said he had gotten the quote from David Boaz at the Cato Institute. Boaz referred me to a paper by Denis Doyle and Terry Hartle, at the time both at the American Enterprise Institute. After all this chummy quoting without citations by right-wing think tanks, it turned out that Doyle and Hartle had estimated the proportion from 1980 census data. It was nowhere near half.

I described my findings in *Education Week* as "George Will's Urban Legend" and, at the suggestion of a friend, sent a prepublication copy to the *Wall Street Journal* editorial page (Bracey, 1993). I received a letter from Daniel Henninger, an op-ed page editor, thanking me for the submission and specifically thanking me for debunking Will's phony statistic. But just before California voted on a voucher proposition that fall, the *Journal* carried a much-longer-than-usual editorial titled "Teacher Knows Best" (*Wall Street Journal,* 1993). The editorial supported the voucher referendum and delivered to its readers Will's phony statistic as if it were real. The disconnect between the *Journal's* reportage, which is often balanced and fair, and its editorial page, has been observed by many other journalists. A writer for the on-line magazine *Slate* once referred to the *Journal's* editorial page as "a viper's nest of right wing vitriol." Another, noting that one article reported that more than half of American corporations pay no federal income tax, wondered if the editors actually read their own paper.

Part III of this book provides a summary of data pertaining to the achievements of American public schools. You need to know this stuff. In Part II, Aspects of Achievement, we'll also provide a brief historical exposition of America's loss of confidence in its schools.

Please note: While Part III focuses on data that pertain to tough questions, considerable data are sprinkled throughout the book, especially in Part I. These data are cross-referenced at the beginning of Part III.

Principles of Data Interpretation, or, How to Keep From Getting Statistically Snookered

This quiz is made up of statements interpreting (or misinterpreting) educational statistics. Give reasons why you think the statements might be true and what you might do to verify their accuracy. Take this quiz now and after you have finished the book. Write your answers down both times for comparison purposes. My responses are given at the end of the book. No peeking.

1. "Home schoolers posted an average ACT score of 22.7 out of a possible 36, tying with students in Rhode Island, who had the highest ACT marks of teens in any state" (Andrea Billups, *Washington Times,* August 18, 1999, p. A3). Students in Virginia scored only 20.6. Any comments on why Rhode Island students would score so high? On why home schoolers would? On why Virginia students would score so low?

2. An item on NPR's "All Things Considered" in August 1999 stated that production in Russia grew 14% in the past 12 months, so the country was clearly headed for recovery. Any comments?

3. "The average SAT score for all students was 1,014 in one year and it was 964 for those saying they were going to major in education. So the average student is 50 SAT points smarter than his teacher" (Martin Gross, author of *The Conspiracy of Ignorance: The Failure of American Public Schools,* in a speech at the Cato Institute, Washington, D.C., September 13, 1999). Any comments?

4. "On virtually every measure, schools are performing more poorly today than 40 years ago" (Martin Gross, same speech). Any comments?

5. A report from the Educational Testing Service (ETS) showed that 2 years after graduation, males with high school grade point averages (GPAs) of 3.0 or higher earned $1,062 a month, while those who had GPAs from 0 to 1.99 made $1,252 a month. The report comments: "While it shows that male undergraduates with the lowest GPAs had higher average earnings than those with the highest GPAs, the difference was not statistically significant." Any comments on the report's comment? (*ETS Policy Notes,* 9(2), Summer, 1999, p. 2).

6. On September 23, 1999, Gannett News Service reported that a survey of mayors found that four out of five of them said that their city had a shortage of workers. Fifty-eight percent of the mayors said that the shortage was affecting their ability to attract new business and 40% said that it was hurting their ability to keep existing businesses in their cities" (Sioux Falls *Argus Leader,* "Worker Shortage Hurts Cities, Mayors Say" [Associated Press wire story], September 23, 1999, p. 9A). Any comments?

7. In 1993, former Secretary of Education William Bennett released a report via the American Legislative Exchange Council contending that money was unrelated to achievement. Bennett observed that some of the states with the highest SAT averages were low spenders while some of those that spent the most money had low SATs. Looking over Bennett's report, columnist George Will pointed out that North Dakota, South Dakota, Iowa, Utah, and

Minnesota were all low spenders with high SAT scores, while New Jersey spent more per child than any other state and finished only 39th among states for SAT averages. Any comments?

8. In the Summer 1999 issue of *Educational Evaluation and Policy Analysis,* University of Rochester economist Eric Hanushek claimed that "the information that we have from 1970 for NAEP [National Assessment of Educational Progress] indicates that our 17-year-olds were performing roughly the same in 1996 as in 1970. . . . There have been improvements in NAEP scores for younger students, but they are not maintained and are not reflected in the skills that students take to college and to the job market. In summary, the overall picture is one of stagnant performance." Any comments?

1

Beware of Averages

We begin with this principle because it is perhaps the first law of statistics. In college, everyone learns a rule: "No measure of central tendency without a measure of variability." The rule is invariably forgotten immediately on leaving statistics class. Virtually all reports deal with either ranks or averages (we will have more to say about ranks later). But averages can mislead. One place we can see that clearly is in the study linking the Third International Mathematics and Science Study (TIMSS) and the National Assessment of Educational Progress (NAEP; Riley, 1998). This study permits comparisons among the 41 nations that participated in TIMSS and the 40-odd states that took part in the 1996 NAEP assessments of mathematics and science.

The "average" score for the United States put us just above the international average in science (58% correct vs. the average of 56%) and just below average in math (53% vs. 55%). But this national average obscures the enormous variability of scores among the different states—not to mention among pupils. At the top, one group of mostly midwestern states had scores almost as high as the highest nations, being exceeded by only 6 of the 41 participating countries in math, and only 1 in science. At the bottom, the lowest-scoring states had scores that were barely above the lowest three countries, in this instance Colombia, Kuwait, and South Africa.

Of course, the scores for each state are also averages. In each state some students scored higher, some lower.

As long as we are considering averages, we should note that statisticians recognize three different ways of measuring an "average": mean, median, and mode. The mode is the most frequently occurring score and is seldom the best descriptor of average. The mean is what most people think of as average: The sum of all scores divided by the number of scores. This statistic for average becomes problematic if there are a few extreme scores. The average income of 100 people would be distorted if one of those people were Bill Gates.

There is a way to render Gates just another guy, and that is with an average defined as the median. The median is the point that divides the scores in half, with 50% of the scores above the median and 50% below. When you're counting scores to find the halfway point, Gates counts the same as anyone else.

The most common means of measuring the variability around the average is called the standard deviation. Its formula is found in any statistics book.

There are ways of displaying average scores and variability simultaneously, and these provide a more complete picture. One common method is called a "box-and-whiskers" display and is shown below:

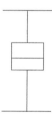

The average score—mean or median—is given by the horizontal line in the middle of the box. The horizontal lines at the top and bottom of the box might be plus or minus one standard deviation or perhaps the 75th and 25th percentiles. The whiskers might be any of several statistics: plus or minus two or three standard deviations or, say, the 5th and 95th percentiles. Whatever index of variability is chosen, this kind of a graph provides a visual representation of how much the scores vary around the average. The TIMSS reports use a variation of this by presenting the average with the various percentiles shown horizontally with different shadings:

The 50th percentile is represented by a box rather than a point because its representation includes a confidence interval. Confidence intervals specify the range in which the true average could occur for the whole population. They are the same kind of notation as occurs when the newspapers present the results of a poll and note that "this poll has a sampling error of plus or minus 4%." Anytime one uses a sample, rather than the whole eligible population—and this is almost all of the time in educational research—one must allow for the possibility that the results obtained are not precisely what one would obtain with a second study. Confidence intervals allow you to specify the possible range of the average score.

NAEP's *Trends in Academic Progress* simply lists the various scores that correspond to the percentiles from 5th to 95th. The main point of the principle, though, is that an average score of any kind—mean, median, or mode—can be misleading when taken alone. Just because the flood waters averaged 2 feet in depth and the citizens averaged 6 feet in height, doesn't mean that nobody drowned.

CHAPTER 2

Follow the Money

Paraphrased: Who benefits? Look for motives.

It is depressing to follow the first principle, which is purely statistical, with this one, which is mostly political or ideological. But in the current context of educational reform, there is a great deal of "research" that is either designed to prove a political stance or is spun to accomplish the same goal.

Thus, every year the American Legislative Exchange Council (ALEC), an organization of conservative legislators, puts out a study to "prove" that there is no relationship between money and achievement. The first such study was issued by former Secretary of Education William Bennett in 1993 and involved only two variables: state level "achievement" as measured by SAT scores and state level per-pupil expenditures (Bennett, 1993).

To start with, one can wonder about the choice of the SAT as a measure of "achievement," especially at the state level. After all, it was born with its middle initial referring to "aptitude," not "assessment," as is the current practice. Its developers considered it to be basically another IQ test and for many years officials at Educational Testing Service contended that the SAT was *impervious* to instruction.

In any case, Bennett conducted no real statistical analyses of the results, but merely pointed out that some of the low-spending states had high SAT scores and some of the high-spending states were ranked relatively low. This kind of "research" is often picked up by ideologically flavored pundits. Thus George Will took to the op-ed page of the *Washington Post* to observe that a number of midwestern states were low spenders and high scorers while New Jersey spent more money per child per year than any other state in the union and still managed to finish only 39th in the Great SAT Race (Will, 1993c).

What neither Will nor Bennett bothered to observe was that in the high-scoring states, virtually no one takes the SAT. In those states some 4% to 10% of the seniors take the SAT because they want to leave the Midwest and attend schools like Stanford on the West Coast or the Ivies on the East Coast, all of which require the SAT.

In New Jersey, on the other hand, in 1993, 76% of the seniors huddled in angst on Saturday mornings to bubble-in answer sheets for the College Board. One might think that New Jersey should be commended for encouraging more than three fourths of its seniors to apply to colleges that require the SAT, but that is not how Will and Bennett saw it.

Will might not have known about the low participation rates for SATs in the Midwest, but Bennett, who, as secretary of education put out the infamous "wall charts," surely did. Those charts divided states into two groups: SAT states and ACT states. It is disturbing to find the author of *The Book of Virtues* so cavalier about two of them, truth and honesty.

In 1996, Brian Powell and Lala Carr Steelman analyzed the relationship between SAT scores and spending while statistically controlling for differences in participation rates among the states (Powell & Steelman, 1996). They reached two principal conclusions: (a) the differences in participation rates account for virtually all differences among states; (b) when differences in participation rates are controlled, total SAT scores rise by 15 points for every $1,000 above the national average a state spends on K-12 education. Thus even a measure as remote from and tangential to everyday instruction as the SAT is shown to be influenced by spending.

Those who have decided for political or ideological reasons that money doesn't matter are unaffected by actual disinterested research. For example, it has been pointed out that Eric Hanushek's conclusions to this effect are contradicted by his own data. In addition, Hanushek has included studies with questionable measures in his analyses and refused to include studies that do indicate a relationship (a summary of these studies can be found in Bracey, 1995d, and Grissmer, 1999).

Hanushek also illustrates the perils of advocacy in his writing about class size, or, more specifically, class size reduction. In spite of the fact that the results from Tennessee's Project STAR have been analyzed by other neutral researchers—and confirmed—Hanushek claims that class size is unrelated to achievement. According to some, Hanushek cannot retreat from this position because he has testified in several court cases. To change his mind in light of new evidence would be to undo those cases.

We can predict, without fear of contradiction, that future research will find that the Florida voucher program "works," that it shows that the market works, that choice improves achievement, and so on. We can predict this because, as with Cleveland, Milwaukee, San Antonio, and New York City, the researcher who hired to evaluate the outcomes is one Paul Peterson of Harvard.

Nota Bene: This is *not* an ad hominem argument against Peterson. Ad hominem arguments are those that connect qualities that are not logically related. Thus, if I said Peterson's results are not to be trusted because he is a noted thespian, I would be making an ad hominem argument. Being a thespian (acting on the stage) is not logically related to the ability to conduct sound research.

The argument against Peterson is based on his writing and on past behavior that bears directly on the issue of the impact of school vouchers. Consider this Peterson statement made long before the latest *Star Wars* movie was even contemplated: "[voucher advocates] are a small band of Jedi attackers, using their intellectual powers to fight the unified might of Death Star forces led by Darth Vader, whose intellectual capacity has been corrupted by the urge for complete hegemony" (Peterson, 1990, p. 73).

This is not the conclusion of a disinterested researcher. This is the statement of a person who has moved from research to advocacy. Peterson refers to himself as a "Jedi warrior." Such a move is perfectly legitimate, of course, but one cannot then continue to pass oneself off as a neutral researcher.

The advocates of vouchers have in the past coordinated their efforts to give vouchers credibility, and we can expect them to continue to do so in the future. Consider their handling of the voucher program in Milwaukee.

Peterson released a "study" indicating that the Milwaukee data show that choice works, it just takes 4 years for the effect to show up. Peterson's claim was not made in an article in a learned journal nor in a paper presented to a scholarly organization. It first appeared as an Associated Press wire story. The story appeared the same day that Peterson and protege Jay P. Greene authored an op-ed essay in the *Wall Street Journal* (Greene & Peterson, 1996). This happened to be the same day that then-presidential candidate Robert Dole addressed the Republican National Convention on education, calling for choice and vouchers. Some coincidence.

Within a few days, both William Bennett and Lamar Alexander had managed to get themselves on national television talk shows plumping Peterson's Milwaukee "findings." Noted pedagogue Rush Limbaugh had already sent them over the airwaves.

Other researchers have been unable to replicate Peterson's findings, in part because it is not clear what statistical procedures he used—in the paper that finally appeared, he does not tell the reader. Cecilia Rouse, an economist at Princeton, found a small positive outcome for the voucher children in math but not in reading. But when she tried to use test scores for the same children for even 2 years, the effect disappeared, meaning that it was tiny and ephemeral indeed (Rouse, 1998).

For his part, Peterson is on record as saying he doesn't trust any voucher evaluations except those that he conducts. Thus his position is not only one of advocacy but one of dismissing all other researchers.

As noted earlier, after one becomes an advocate for a particular position one cannot present oneself as a neutral researcher.

"Follow the money" was the advice given to Robert Woodward and Carl Bernstein by "Deepthroat," their principal informant, as they pursued their investigation of the matter that came to be called simply, "Watergate." It is unfortunate that ideology and politics have infected the area of educational research, but in many areas they have (phonics vs. whole language is another arena). The wise reader of research would do well to look for motives and agendas and funding sources.

When one looks for the funding of many school critics, one often finds a conservative foundation such as Bradley, Olin, or Scaife. As the National Committee for Responsive Philanthropy pointed out, some one dozen foundations have pushed the discussion of social issues to the Right. While "mainstream" foundations such as Rockefeller, Ford, or MacArthur were acting in a pragmatic and issue-oriented way, the conservative foundations were generally funding anyone who claimed to be against "liberal big governmentism" (National Committee for Responsive Philanthropy, 1997).

3

Beware of the Uncritical Acceptance of Convenient Conclusions

Whether by yourself or by someone else. This book is all about *your* handling of data, but you've got to be wary of how others handle it. In the previous section we found William Bennett, Lamar Alexander, and Rush Limbaugh accepting the conclusions of a study that they could not possibly have known were right or wrong: When Paul Peterson first released the Milwaukee data, his paper included no indication of the methods he had followed or what statistical procedures he used. At one point, he appears to have used statistical analyses he had earlier said were not needed.

At least in the Milwaukee case, Peterson himself had gone over the data with a fine-toothed analytical comb. Yet Peterson stood before an audience in March 1999 and noted that the longer American students stay in school, the farther they fall behind their international peers. Such a statement could be reached only by an uncritical acceptance of the TIMSS (Third International Math and Science Study) final year study, a study that has been critiqued soundly for its numerous methodological flaws (Bracey, 1998b, 1998c; Rotberg, 1998).

The reader should not assume it is only the denizens of the Right that uncritically welcome data that favor their position. *The Manufactured Crisis* by David Berliner and Bruce Biddle (1995) contains few errors, but there are a couple. The authors quote the Directors of the Iowa Testing Programs as stating that "composite achievement [on the Iowa Tests of Basic Skills] in 1984-85 was at an all-time high in nearly all test areas" (p. 33). They then go on to write,

> Given these data, we wonder where the columnist James J. Kilpatrick got his information when he asserted, "The average achievement of high school students on most standardized tests is now lower than it was 26 years ago when Sputnik was launched." Mr. Kilpatrick, like so many of the critics, seems to have been unencumbered by the facts. In contrast, the evidence from the commercial tests indicates that student achievement has been steadily improving over the years. (p. 33)

Actually, in this case, Kilpatrick is right. Kilpatrick's statement is taken verbatim from *A Nation At Risk* (National Commission on Excellence in Education, 1983). It refers to high school students. The Iowa Tests of Basic Skills (ITBS) cited by Berliner and Biddle are found in the elementary and middle school grades. What had actually happened was that test scores had *not* "been steadily improving over the years." Tracking of ITBS scores usually begins in 1955 when major changes were made in the tests' content (the data actually go back to the 1930s). Test scores rose until about 1965, then dropped for a decade until 1975, then reversed and climbed to record levels by the mid- to late-1980s (depending on grade).

The most recent data that the commissioners assembling *A Nation At Risk* in 1982 (it was published in April, 1983) would have had would have been for the year 1981-1982. Scores for high school students that year were indeed lower than in 1957 when Sputnik was launched, but just barely. Moreover, scores in 1957 were relatively high compared to the levels to which they would fall, but, of course, the implication the commissioners wished to make was that schools were bad back then and conditions had deteriorated since.

If one looks at the whole set of test score trend lines, the commissioners writing *A Nation at Risk* were putting their own spin on the data favorable to their conclusion. They could have written that "test scores have been rising now for seven consecutive years," but this would have been the "glass-is-half-full" interpretation, and the commissioners were definitely considering only empties. Moreover, the commissioners limited their comment to high school students. If they had included elementary and middle school grades, it would not have been true. In any case, it appears that Berliner and Biddle's enthusiasm for their cause led them to be a bit too accepting of data that should have gotten a closer look.

COROLLARY: BEWARE OF CONVENIENT CLAIMS THAT THE SCHOOLS ARE TO BLAME.

In the above we noted that test scores fell from about 1965 to about 1975. That decade began with the Watts riots in Los Angeles. From there, violence spread to virtually every large urban area. During this decade, television came to permeate our homes. Recreational drug use became popular. The decade included Woodstock, Altamont, the summer of love, the Beatles, the Stones, Students for a Democratic Society, the Black Panthers, and the Student Non-Violent Coordinating Committee. It included Vietnam and the Vietnam moratorium movement. It included Kent State, the Chicago Police Riot, and Watergate. It included the assassinations of Robert F. Kennedy, Jr., Martin Luther King, Jr., and Malcolm X. It included the Civil Rights Movement and the Women's Rights Movement. In connection with Vietnam, a popular song of the time included the refrain, "Ain't no time to wonder why, whoopee, we're all gonna die." In such an era, people probably paid less attention to factoring equations and parsing sentences than before or after.

Since the loss of innocence in that decade and subsequent events at home and abroad, we have a hard time remembering what the social context was like pre-Watts. We had just come through the "togetherness" period of the Eisenhower administration. Comedian-commentator Steve Allen had a regular television show and sometimes featured an increasingly looking-for-work comedian named Lenny Bruce. In one episode, Bruce announced to the audience that he was going to give them a four-letter word that began with *s* and ended with *t*. The word was *snot*. The program's censors killed it. Allen made a taped introduction telling the audience that they really wouldn't be shocked. The censors still killed it.

4

Watch for Selectivity
in the Data

You might think that selectivity is hard to spot. After all, you, the reader of research, can see only what the author chooses to reveal. That is true, but on many occasions your knowledge of the field will clearly suggest that the whole story is not there. And there are other occasions where the simple application of logic and/or questioning will indicate that the whole picture is not being shown. Some examples.

Conservative reformers are fond of pointing out that, over a period of time, the proportion of students scoring high on the SAT verbal declined (usually presented as those above 650, sometimes 700; in the original scaling, 650 corresponded to the 93rd percentile, 700 to the 98th). They have used this decline as evidence that the high school curriculum has been dumbed down. In one interesting twist, Richard Herrnstein and Charles Murray argued in *The Bell Curve* that the SAT decline did *not* mean that the average student was learning less (Herrnstein & Murray, 1994). They pointed to the steadiness of PSAT (Preliminary SAT) trends as evidence.

The SAT has forever been a voluntary test taken by a self-selecting sample, those who want to attend colleges and universities that require the test for admission. For the PSAT, however, ETS (Educational Testing Service) would periodically obtain data from national norming studies. A national norming study attempts to obtain a sample that is representative of the nation as a whole. All during the period of the decline of the SAT average score (1963-1980) the PSAT national norming studies show no indication of any fall in that test. Herrnstein and Murray argued that this meant that the average student was doing as well as ever. To them, that in turn implied that the SAT fall reflected a disastrous dumbing down of the curriculum for college-bound students.

There is, of course, a mathematics (neé quantitative) section to the SAT. One can wonder why the reformers consistently report changes in the verbal but not the mathematics section. Could it be because the trends on the SAT-M cannot be used for the same ideological purposes as the SAT-V? The average score on the mathematics test never showed the large decline that the verbal test did, nor did the proportion of high scorers tail off much. In 1981, when the proportion of students scoring above 650 on the SAT-V was almost at its nadir, so was the SAT-M. But that proportion for the SAT-M was still *higher* than it was for the elite group of students who set the standards for the SAT in 1941.[1]

One would think that if the schools were declining, both sections of the test would be equally affected. There is likely some truth to Diane Ravitch's contention that it is easier to dumb down an English course than an algebra course. Easier-to-read books can replace difficult ones, but it's hard to find a substitute formula for solving quadratic equations. Then, too, ever since Sputnik in 1957, and especially since *A Nation At Risk,* math and science have received additional attention in terms of their putative importance to national security, national economic prosperity, and job status. Still, it is hard to imagine that these factors produce such large differences between SAT-M and SAT-V trends.

What the growth in the proportion of high-scoring students on the SAT-M *cannot* be attributed to is the increasing presence of Asian American students. Asian Americans, it is true, score substantially higher than other ethnic groups on the SAT-M. However, they remain too few in number to account for much of the growth. For instance, from 1981 to 1995, the overall proportion of students scoring above 650 grew by 75%. If Asian students are removed from the test-taking pool, the growth falls, but only to 57%.

The SAT-V, though, is something else. As readers might recall, the SAT-V has been accused of class and ethnic bias for containing such words as *regatta*. The SAT-V is largely a *literary* verbal test. The SAT-V decline began in 1963. By 1963, television had become ubiquitous in American households. While television has probably

TABLE 4.1   SAT High Scorers (Percentage Over 650)

Year	Verbal	Math
1981	3.0	7.1
1982	3.0	7.3
1983	2.9	7.9
1984	3.0	8.6
1985	3.6	8.6
.		
.		
.		
1991	3.2	9.7
1992	3.2	10.1
1993	3.4	10.5
1994	3.2	10.6
1995	3.7	12.4
1996	3.6	12.0
1997	4.0	12.4

NOTE: 1996 and 1997 data converted by ETS from recentered scale back to original scale.

increased the daily working vocabulary of Americans, it has had a devastating impact on literary vocabulary.

Table 4.1 shows the proportion of students scoring above 650 on the two sections of the SAT over a 25-year period. Note that the proportion scoring high on the SAT-V has risen in recent years. The critics have had little to say about this.

Here's another example: "There was a steady decline in science achievement scores of U.S. 17-year-olds as measured by national assessments of science in 1969, 1973, and 1977." This is one of 13 "Indicators of the Risk" in *A Nation At Risk*. The evidence of selectivity? The statement applies only to science and then only for science scores for 17-year-olds. One wonders—one *should* wonder anyway—what the rest of the scores look like.

The rest of the scores look like the three parts of Figure 4.1. As can be seen, within the science assessment, only 17-year-olds show the "steady decline." And even that is hypothetical—in the early assessments, NAEP (National Assessment of Educational Progress) was not constructed to provide longitudinal data. The broken lines are statistical estimates for what scores would have been had NAEP been established to provide trends from its inception.

Looking at the trendlines for reading and mathematics, one cannot find any indication of a decline at any of the three ages assessed

Figure 4.1. Trends in Average Scale Scores for the Nation

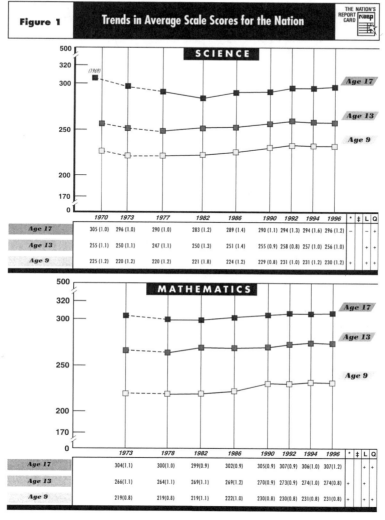

(continued)

by NAEP. Thus, the National Commission on Excellence in Education, the group that produced *A Nation At Risk,* was in possession of nine trendlines—three subject areas and three ages in each subject. Only one of those trendlines could be used to support the crisis rhetoric of *Risk,* so that was the only one that was reported.

The other 12 indicators, by the way, are a golden treasury of selective, spun, and over-simplified statistics—except in two instances where I have not been able to find *any* data to support the allegation.[2]

Figure 4.1. Trends in Average Scale Scores for the Nation *(continued)*

Figure 1 (continued)	**Trends in Average Scale Scores for the Nation**	THE NATION'S REPORT CARD naep

READING

	1971	1975	1980	1984	1988	1990	1992	1994	1996	*	‡	L	Q
Age 17	285(1.2)	286(0.8)	286(1.2)	289(0.6)	290(1.0)	290(1.1)	290(1.1)	288(1.3)	287(1.1)			+	–
Age 13	255(0.9)	256(0.8)	259(0.9)	257(0.5)	258(1.0)	257(0.8)	260(1.2)	258(0.9)	259(0.9)	+		+	
Age 9	208(1.0)	210(0.7)	215(1.0)	211(0.7)	212(1.1)	209(1.2)	211(0.9)	211(1.2)	212(1.0)	+			–

SOURCE: National Center for Education Statistics, National Assessment of Educational Progress (NAEP), 1996 Long-Term Trend Assessment.

NOTE: Standard errors of the estimated scale scores appear in parentheses. [—] Extrapolated from previous NAEP analyses.

* Indicates that the average scale score in 1996 is significantly larger (+) or smaller (–) than the first assessment year.

† Indicates that the average scale score in 1996 is significantly larger (+) or smaller (–) than that in 1994.

L Indicates that the positive (+) or negative (–) linear trend is significant.

Q indicates that the positive (+) or negative (–) quadratic trend is significant.

NOTES

1. The standards for the SAT were set in 1941 by 10,654 students mostly living in the Northeast and mostly planning to attend private Ivy League, Seven Sisters, and other northeastern universities. Ninety-eight percent of the students were white, 61% were male, and fully 41% had attended private, college-preparatory high schools. Currently, a third of

the SAT takers are minorities, 53% are female, and 83% attended public schools.

2. These two are, "Over half the population of gifted students do not match their tested ability with comparable achievement in school," and "Average tested achievement of students graduating from college is also lower." Conversations with both people who acted as staff to the Commission and with Commissioners themselves have failed to uncover the sources of these contentions. On their face, they seem improbable: Achievement tests are the most common instrument used to identify gifted students. Thus, by definition, "gifted" students are matching their ability with achievement. The United States has never had any kind of program to determine the "average tested achievement" of college graduates.

CHAPTER 5

Show Me the Data!

If you encounter unsubstantiated claims, ask to see data or a citation where you can find the data.

It must be wonderful to be a columnist as opposed to, say, a researcher. Researchers have to be prepared to certify everything they claim, either with their own data or those from other studies. Failure to do so results in total loss of credibility.

Columnists never have to document their citations, at least in their columns. Some can. Some can't. Robert Samuelson of *Newsweek* and the *Washington Post* always has a reference handy when I call. On the other hand, I've already documented the second- and third-source nature of some of George Will's claims.

Journalists are, of course, not the only ones to make insupportable claims. Such contentions are the staff of life for politicians. And even some educators.

In the fall of 1995, Bill Clinton and Al Gore sent a letter to the editor of *USA Today* as part of their agenda for getting the schools wired and providing more computer literacy for teachers. In the letter, they claimed that "by 2000, 60% of all jobs will require advanced technological skills." They cited no sources for their claim.

I wrote Messrs. Clinton and Gore asking for a reference for the 60% figure along with a definition of "advanced technological skills." To improve my chances of getting a response, I sent copies of the letter to Secretary of Education Richard Riley and to then-Secretary of Labor Robert Reich. My four epistles produced one reply: Someone in Riley's office wrote to say that she was sure that someone in Reich's office could answer my question. The 60% figure did not accord with projections from the Bureau of Labor Statistics (1997), so I called over there. An official chuckled "If they mean just sitting in front of a PC, maybe so," he said.

On occasion, when you do show the data, someone might challenge, if not its veracity, then its composition and import. For example, in late 1995, I wrote an op-ed essay for the *Washington Post* in which I stated that the proportion of students scoring above 650 on the SAT Mathematics was at a record high and had grown by 75% since 1981 (Bracey, 1995d). In the education chapter of *Issues '96: The Candidate's Briefing Book,* a Heritage Foundation publication for conservative candidates for political office, Denis Doyle (1996) took umbrage at my statistic: "[Bracey] does not tell the reader who is pushing the scores up, mostly Asian and Asian-American students." Doyle presented no data, he only challenged the composition of mine.

In the research community, a contention without evidence is, at best, a hypothesis. Hypotheses can be tested for validity. A call to the College Board (followed by a check) produced a tome of SAT data by ethnicity. If Doyle were right, that the growth was accounted for mostly by Asian American kids, then removing them from the sample should cause the 75% growth figure to disappear or, at least, become quite small. It didn't. It fell to 57%. Asian kids had indeed accounted for *some* of the growth in high scorers. But black, white, Hispanic, and Native American high scorers had grown by 57%, some 76% of the total growth.

The use of cooked or confabulated numbers seems most rampant among "motivational speakers." In the "Fifth Bracey Report on the Condition of Public Education" (Bracey, 1995a) I took a certain Willard Daggett to task for making up some research, then making up more research to explain the first batch of nonexistent research, and making up the organization that supposedly conducted the second bit of research. Daggett continues this practice. In a 1998 speech in Grosse Pointe, Michigan, he created at least 15 nonexistent statistics in the course of an hour's talk. I say at least 15, because I did not bother to track down come claims, such as the one about serving on a commission with Michael Eisner, Bill Gates, and Michael Milken or the one about Stanford growing tomatoes in the Antarctic. Those that I did track down earned Daggett the Who Cares About Facts?, 1 of 11 Rotten Apple awards in the "Ninth Bracey Report on the Condition of Public Education" (Bracey, 1999b).

Some people will fake knowledge to impress and convince you. Others will create stuff to intimidate you into silence. In a school district where I once worked, a new superintendent would often begin sentences at faculty meetings with, "What the research says is . . ." When I first heard such comments, I was ecstatic. I'm a researcher. This is my kind of guy. But it didn't take long to realize he didn't have a clue what the research said. It was a ploy to stave off any potential disputations. The faculty in this district were pretty independent thinkers. A statement presented as the superintendent's allegation might well be challenged. But no one was going to contest a statement that bore the weight of what THE RESEARCH said.

Beyond the outright fakers, there are people, probably a majority of the citizenry, who make assertions predicated on conclusions they have heard stated over and over or on things that everyone just *knows* are true. As a variation on asking for data, you might inquire of people, "How do you know that?" You will likely be surprised at how little knowledge rests on a solid foundation of data, how much of it cannot be tracked to a specific source.

A caution though: I ask "How do you know that?" a lot because, as a researcher, it is simply part of my culture. Most people are not researchers and are not used to having to warrant their knowledge in some way. Some people are likely to perceive the question as a threat, as asking them to justify their existence, even. Be gentle.

In the movie *Jerry Maguire,* Tom Cruise plays a sports agent for a football star, played by Cuba Gooding, Jr. Cruise has an epiphany and concludes a high salary is not all that important. Gooding still thinks otherwise and as Cruise reveals the contract he has gotten for Gooding, Gooding keeps shouting, "Show me the money!" When you see an unsubstantiated allegation, say "Show me the data!" If they can't, don't listen to 'em.

6

Beware of Nostalgia

Nostalgia, by itself, is dangerous. Nostalgia blended with our all-too-fallible memories produces a dangerous mix, indeed. Nostalgic thinking pervades thinking about public schools.

At one point, while taping a National Public Radio show with John Merrow, Merrow thrust a small book into my hands. "Do you think today's students can handle these kinds of problems?" he asked. They were two-step math problems. I demurred, not being a curriculum expert. Merrow went on: "These are the kinds of problems my grandfather handled routinely as an eighth grader." I pointed out that when John's grandfather was an eighth grader, a lot of his age mates would have already departed school. The topic then changed.

After the program ended, I noticed a young woman hanging back until all of the rest of the audience who had comments or questions for me had finished. She then approached and she, too, thrust a book in my hands. "Are these the kind of problems he was talking about?" They were. I said "Yes, where did you get that book?"

"It's my book," she said. "I'm an eighth grader."

Just when nostalgia began to afflict thinking about public schools is not altogether clear, but when I was researching the history of educational reform for the book *Final Exam* (Bracey, 1995b), I began to notice it shortly after the end of World War II. It is in this period that the frequency and intensity of criticism of public schools increased. Arthur Bestor, for example, subtitled his influential 1953 book, *Educational Wastelands,* "The *Retreat* From Learning in Our Public Schools (emphasis added).

Similarly, in his 1958 essay in *Life* magazine's five-part post-Sputnik series on "Crisis in Education," novelist Sloan Wilson (1958) declared that our schools, "which were supposed to reflect one of history's most noble ideals and to cultivate the nation's youthful minds have degenerated into a system for coddling and entertaining the mediocre" (pp. 31-32; also see "Crisis in Education," 1958).

People's nostalgia for the good old days colors how they perceive data emanating from today's schools. Bestor, for example, was at pains to point out that 50 years before his book, half of the high school seniors took Latin and Greek while today (1953), fewer than a quarter took any language at all. For a historian, this was a notable historical lapse. A historian, one might have thought, would have taken care to make sure that the conditions of 50 years earlier were comparable to "today's." Of course, they were not. In Bestor's day, the high school completion rate was approaching 65%; 50 years earlier it had been barely 10%.

In his 1989 memoir, *The Thirteenth Man,* the first secretary of education, Terrel Bell (1988), wondered, "how do we get back to being a nation of learners?" We have never been a nation of learners, of course, and many data would argue that we are closer to such a state today than at any prior time.

The nostalgia of today for an earlier time and the nostalgia of the 1950s for a still earlier time leads to an interesting logical sequence: If today's students are learning less than their parents, and if their parents in turn learned less than *their* parents, if we go back in time far enough, we should reach a point where everyone learned. This, of course, is quite the opposite of the point we do reach. There are not a lot of data that bear on the performance of schools over a long period of time. The existing, long-term relevant test score data indicate that scores rose from about 1955 to about 1965, fell for about a decade, then recovered to reach all-time highs around 1990. The scores remain today at these highs (these data are discussed in detail in Chapter 25).

Another telling bit of information on the good old days comes from the *New York Times.* Through the history department at Columbia University, the *Times* commissioned a survey of history and geography knowledge of college freshmen. It was quite aghast at what it found:

A large majority of the students showed that they had no knowledge of elementary aspects of American history. They could not identify such names as Abraham Lincoln, Thomas Jefferson, Andrew Jackson, or Theodore Roosevelt. . . . Most of our students do not have the faintest notion of what this country looks like. St. Louis was placed on the Pacific Ocean, Lake Huron, Lake Erie, the Atlantic Ocean, Ohio River, St. Lawrence River, and almost every place else. (Fine, 1943, p. 1)

The *Times* was incensed. It ran the story on a Sunday on page 1. The story sat next to the other major story of the day, "Patton Attacks East of El Guettar"—April 4, 1943. What makes the story particularly scandalous was that the students in question were not high schoolers but college freshmen.

Consider for a moment that in 1943 the high school graduation rate was about 45%. Of these, some 15% would go on to college. Thus, presumably the most academically elite 7% of our students (45% 15%) were seen to be merely an elite group of ignoramuses— "presumably," because as David Owen and Nicholas Lemann have observed, Ivy League schools in the 1930s and 1940s were country clubs (Owen, 1995; Lemann, 1998).

Given the task of identifying Walt Whitman, students named him as a missionary to the Far East, a pioneer, a colonizer, an explorer, a speculator, an unpatriotic writer, a humorist, a musician, a composer, a famous cartoonist, the father of blank verse, an English poet, and a columnist. "Hundreds of students," sniffed the *Times*, "listed Whitman as being an orchestra leader." The Gray Lady showed no hint of expertise in contemporary cultural literacy: she failed to note that Paul Whiteman was a popular jazz bandleader of the day.

A COROLLARY PRINCIPLE TO BEWARE OF NOSTALGIA: BEWARE OF COMMENTS ABOUT KNOW-NOTHING KIDS.

I believe there might be something hard-wired in the human brain that activates in most people around age 40 and says the coming crop of kids doesn't know anything. The first "Bracey Report" was not called that because I had no intention at the time of writing a series of studies. It was called "Why Can't They Be Like We Were?" (Bracey, 1991b). That is a snippet of a lyric from a 1960 musical, *Bye Bye Birdie*. The complete refrain goes, "Oh, why can't they be like we were, perfect in every way? Oh, what's the matter with kids today?"

1960. Forty years ago.

If anything, attitudes have hardened in recent years. Pollster Daniel Yankelovich reported in 1998 that,

> A trend toward Social Darwinism shows up clearly in my firm's annual tracking of studies of social change. Our data reveal a shift away from the kind of egalitarianism dominant in the 1960s and 1970s which assumed that everyone was entitled to share in the bounty of available resources, even if this required large-scale redistribution. The assumption then was that un-equal results were society's fault, and that it was society's obligation to address and correct them. We are now moving back toward the traditional American value that people are responsible for their own lives, and that the reality of life is that there will inevitably be winners and losers. (Yankelovich, 1998, p. 28)

Along with this austere attitude toward what society owes the individual is an increase in negative attitudes about youth. When Public Agenda (1999) surveyed people about "kids these days" in 1996, 67% of the respondents used words such as *rude, irresponsible,* and *wild* to describe teenagers. By 1999 the figure was 71% for the general public and 74% for parents.

So "know-nothing kids" comments might simply reflect general patterns, but these patterns affect the attitudes people bring to the interpretation of data.

But the data indicate that, if anything, kids today know more than ever. These data can be anecdotal, quasi-formal, or formal. Anecdotally, my children learned biology in terms of DNA, genetics, evolution, ecology, and so on. I memorized phyla. Semiformally, they peruse the sample science items in *Science Achievement in the Middle School Years,* the TIMSS eighth-grade science report (Beaton, Martin, Mullis et al., 1996). Who in our generation could have coped with these questions as eighth graders? One question asks, "What is the main function of chloroplasts in a plant cell?" Chloro-what? (For the record, my computer is a late 1998 model and its spell-checker doesn't know either). Another labels six items in an aquarium and asks the student to "Explain why each of the following is important in maintaining the ecosystem." The eco-what?

A "Sally Forth" cartoon strip some years ago captured the real historical trends well. Hilary, the Forth's daughter, advises her parents, "Our teacher said we might need a little help with our social studies project."

Sally enquires, "What's your project?"

"We get two choices. The first is build a working model of the Panama Canal."

Sally is incredulous: "What's the second? Construct a relief map of the Andes?"

"How did you know?"

Now husband Ted chimes in: "What happened to the good old days? My fourth grade social studies project was to list North Carolina's natural resources."

(I did that. I listed them for China later and I even listed them for something called Assyria.)

I thought this strip was funny when I first read it. Now it seems altogether too grimly accurate. Consider these standards, the first a 10th-grade social studies standard from Virginia, the second a 6th-grade standard from South Dakota:

The student will analyze the regional development of Asia, Africa, the Middle East, Latin America, and the Caribbean in terms of physical, economic, and cultural characteristics and historical evolution from 1000 A.D. to the present.

Students will analyze the geographic, political, economic, and social structures of the early civilization of ancient Greece with emphasis on the location and physical setting that supported the rise of this civilization; the connections between geography and the development of city-states, including patterns of trade and commerce; the transition from tyranny to oligarchy to early democratic patterns of citizenship; the differences between Athenian direct democracy and representative democracy; the significance of Greek mythology in the everyday life of people in ancient Greece and its influence on modern literature and language; the similarities and differences between life in Athens and Sparta; the rise of Alexander the Great in the

north and the spread of Greek culture; and the cultural contri-
butions in the areas of art, science, language, architecture, government and philosophy.

The formal data pertaining to achievement over time are summa-
rized in Chapter 25 in Part III.

The know-nothing attitudes have been abetted, unfortunately,
by many reports such as *A Nation at Risk* claiming that American
schools are in crisis and by media misreporting on such events as
TIMSS. When the TIMSS eighth-grade results emerged, American
kids were average in both math and science. The had an average of
53% correct in math and 58% correct in science. The international
average for all 41 nations was 55% and 56%, respectively. All
but two newspapers (*Education Week* and the *New York Times*)
changed "average" to "mediocre." Average is a statistic, mediocre is
a judgment.

One newspaper, the *Louisville Courier-Journal,* devoted 15
paragraphs to the study. Fourteen of the 15 were devoted to the
slightly-less-than-average score in math, one acknowledged the
slightly-above-average finish in science.

When the TIMSS Final Year report appeared, the media universally portrayed it as an apples-to-apples comparison in which our
12th graders got stomped by other countries' 12th graders and in
which our best 12th graders got stomped by everyone else's best
12th graders. But, as described in Chapter 24 in Part III, the TIMSS
Final Year study wasn't even an apples-to-oranges comparison. It
was more like apples to aardvarks (Mullis et al., 1998).

There have, unfortunately, been data from education itself that
have appeared to corroborate know-nothing attitudes. These have
come from NAEP. The original intent for NAEP was descriptive.
The plan was to ask some questions that 50% of respondents were
expected to get right, some questions that only 10% would get
right, and some questions that 90% would get right. In this way the
founders of NAEP hoped to paint a picture of what most people
knew, what some people knew, and what very few people knew. Any
judgments about whether the results were good, bad, or indifferent
would be left to others. NAEP was to discover the incidence of
knowledge just as a health department might describe fitness or the
incidence of tuberculosis.

After the formation of the National Assessment Governing Board
(NAGB, pronounced NAG-bee), ideologically driven attempts were

made to make NAEP not *descriptive,* but *prescriptive.* It was now to prescribe what students *should* know and to set standards in terms of performance levels described as Basic, Proficient, and Advanced. The NAGB ideologues wanted to use these standards to sustain the sense of crisis established by *A Nation at Risk.* Their first attempt at such standard setting produced standards that were so ridiculously high that even the ideologues backed off. They later hired a team of first-rate evaluators who told them that the standard setting process did not work. NAGB summarily fired the team.[1]

To get an idea of the unreasonableness of the standards, we can note that in the 1996 NAEP science assessment, only 18% of fourth graders scored at the Proficient level, and only 2% attained the rarefied level of Advanced. Yet, when these same fourth graders went up against their peers in 25 other nations, they finished third.

The NAEP standards that are universally reported by the media are universally rejected by psychometricians. Studies of the standards by the General Accounting Office, the Center for Research in Evaluation, Standards and Student Testing (CRESST), and Lyle V. Jones of the University of North Carolina at Chapel Hill have all found the standards wanting. In a speech delivered at Educational Testing Service (which houses NAEP), Jones (1998) said flatly that, "Efforts to fix cut scores in NAEP to separate achievement levels, Basic, Proficient, and Advanced, have not been successful."

It is unfortunate that the education reporters are so willing to be critical about schools and so unwilling to approach critically things like the NAEP proficiency levels. Despite all of the criticisms, I have never seen any NAEP coverage even note that the levels are suspect. Fortunately, the National Research Council has called for their abolition (Pellegrino, Jones, & Mitchell, 1999).

NOTE

1. At least, they tried to. The contract, as it turned out, forbade such dismissal. The team was led by Daniel Stufflebeam of Western Michigan University. The other members were Richard Jaeger of the University of North Carolina at Greensboro and Michael Scriven, at the time also of Western Michigan.

CHAPTER 7

Beware of Causal Explanations Made From Correlational Data

Most educational research deals with correlational data.

Whether or not the human brain is hard wired to make "know-nothing" inferences about the next generation of kids, it sure appears to be wired to infer causality from correlations among phenomena in the world. The British Empiricist philosopher David Hume (1711-1776) laid out the conditions under which humans say that one event causes another. Mostly it has to do with time and repetition. If Event A is always followed within a certain time by Event B, we tend to say that A caused B to happen.

People infer causation from correlation often, especially when the data are convenient to a predisposed attitude. For instance, in the field of education, the California legislature mandated "whole language." On a NAEP (National Assessment of Educational Progress) reading assessment about 5 years later, California's reading scores dropped. Aha, said phonics proponents. The drop was caused by the disastrous adoption of whole language. The issue played much larger than just a war over learning to read. For some reason, phonics has become the poster child of the Right and most of the causal inferences were made from that wing of the political spectrum.

Was the fall *caused* by whole language? If it was so, surely it was a historical moment. It would have been the first time in history that a top-down mandate from a state legislature had been immediately and universally adopted by the teachers and administrators. Those who are almost universally held by critics to be impervious to change—public school teachers and administrators—rolled over and docilely not only accepted the new law, but incorporated it into their pedagogy. In a pig's eye.

Certainly this had never happened in California before, even with a slowly developed change. Some years ago, California developed "curriculum frameworks" for teaching various subjects. Little money was appropriated for staff development to familiarize teachers with what the frameworks implied about what should be taught and how.

David Cohen, then at Michigan State, and a group of his colleagues were hired to study how well the schools had put the mathematics framework in place (Cohen, 1990). Cohen's team found teachers all over the place in terms of how they interpreted the framework. Some felt it justified what they had been doing all along, even when it "outlined a vision of practice that might suggest a fundamentally different classroom epistemology than the one they enact." Some were uncertain how to change to make their teaching line up with the framework. Some recognized that their teaching conflicted with the framework, but continued to teach the way they always had because they felt they had been successful. Some simply ignored the new framework. And some teachers pointed out that the new framework tried to teach teachers with the very same pedagogy it told them to stop using with kids.

Given the plethora of interpretations, it is unlikely that many of California's teachers stopped teaching reading the way they always had the day the law prescribing whole language went into effect.

When one looks at the state-by-state NAEP reading results for the year of California's drop, one notices that virtually all of the participating states also experienced a decline. For six of them, Delaware, Louisiana, New Mexico, Pennsylvania, South Carolina, and Virginia, the drop was larger than in California. Yet, none of these states were indicted for teaching whole language. California was simply a convenient target for the Right.

A decline in NAEP scores for most states suggests another causal explanation: a technical glitch in the procedure that equates the new test with the old. Indeed, in the 1998 NAEP reading assessment, virtually all of the states had increases back to the previous reading levels. This is additional evidence of an earlier technical aberration.

There are other inappropriate causal inferences that are not tinged with ideology. For instance, in the early 1990s the College Board announced that algebra was a "gatekeeper" course. That is, students who took algebra, especially those who took it in the eighth or ninth grades, tended to take rigorous high school curricula and to go on to college. Causality was clearly implied and in some places, such as Milwaukee, moves were made to require early algebra for all students.

In January 1998, the U.S. Department of Education joined the algebra bandwagon. It declared that, "The latest research shows that taking rigorous mathematics courses such as algebra and geometry early in secondary schools is a gateway to college and future employment" (Riley, 1998, p. 1). The idea put forth was that if we can just get everyone to take algebra early on, everyone will make it to college.

The College Board and the Department had noticed a correlation: There is a correlation between taking algebra early and ending up in college. They turned it into a causal explanation: *Because* these kids took algebra early, they were impelled toward rigor and higher learning.

There is, of course, another explanation. Kids exist independent of their test scores. They are known to their teachers and principals and counselors. American schools track kids based on ability (even when they say they don't). It seems likely that those kids who end up in algebra in eighth or ninth grade are those students the school has identified as material for the college-bound curriculum.

Without additional evidence, we cannot decide between the two explanations above, and there might be other explanations we haven't yet noticed. Additional evidence would come from observing those who would not have been coached into algebra but who, for one reason or another, had it imposed on them. If algebra is indeed the gatekeeper, once these kids get through the gate we should see them taking a rigorous curriculum and heading for college. Or getting better jobs. Or maybe dropping out in greater numbers: Imposing algebra on the unsuspecting might turn off as many kids as it turns on.

There is some evidence, unfortunately not complete, from Milwaukee. In 1993-1994, Milwaukee instituted an algebra-for-all program. Prior to that year, only 35% of the students took algebra in the ninth grade. The failure rate for algebra rose from 40% to 47%, not a huge increase. One is left with two conclusions: Either algebra is easier than previously thought or the course was watered down to accommodate children of lesser ability.

Collateral evidence of the impact of algebra in Milwaukee is not overwhelming. Prior to the algebra-for-all regime, 37% of all graduates said they planned to attend college. In 1997, the figure was 43%, only a small increase. More students in Milwaukee signed up for Advanced Placement (AP) mathematics courses, but only a few more took AP exams and a higher proportion of those failed to obtain at least a "3," the minimum passing grade on the 5-point AP scale. The algebra requirement does not seem to have increased the proportion of minority students taking AP tests. Data on dropout rates are not available, but there has been an increase in the proportion of students who are not declared to be 10th graders at the end of the ninth grade, presumably because failing algebra prevented them from obtaining enough credits.

From an evolutionary standpoint, seeing causality from correlation is probably, by and large, a good thing. It stimulates us to investigate patterns of events in the environment. But we must investigate further to see if the patterns are causally linked. Too often, we make the causal inference without these further investigations.

In educational research, one of the most common statistics is the correlation coefficient or, to be precise, the Pearson Product-Moment Correlation Coefficient. It can be applied to any two variables. The resulting coefficient does not link the two variables causally and might not even be meaningful. Before everyone started wearing jeans, there was a correlation between the stock market and hemlines. Short skirts meant prosperity. To the best of my knowledge, no one ever suggested that dress manufacturers raise hems as a means of stimulating the economy, although it is theoretically possible that the resulting increases in testosterone levels might have been sublimated into higher productivity.

Similarly, there is a correlation in election years between which conference wins the Super Bowl and which party wins the presidency. All you need for a correlation coefficient are two variables and the statistical formula.

Closely related to the problem of inferring causality from correlation is the error known technically as the "base rates fallacy." Base rates fallacy is a formal way of talking about an error. The error occurs when one makes a causal statement based on observations of a sample without checking to see what's happening in the whole population—the whole population is the "base."

Probably the most famous example of the base rates fallacy comes from the early days of psychiatry when someone decided that schizophrenia was caused by brain damage. The clinician in question had performed autopsies on the brains of schizophrenics and noticed brain damage in more than 90% of them. Aha! Brain damage causes schizophrenia. The problem was, if the clinician had checked the incidence of brain damage in normal people (the base) of the same age as the schizophrenics, he would have found damage in more than 90% of them as well.

The base rates fallacy is not limited to arcane observations from autopsies. At the 1997 convention of the American Educational Research Association, one presentation analyzed the characteristics of the five nations that had scored high in the eighth-grade mathematics tests of TIMSS (Mullis, 1997). All of them had highly centralized education systems. Aha! Centralized education is important to scoring well in international comparisons. Perhaps the United States needs to establish national standards.

This is a conclusion based on a sample, 5 nations, not the whole population. In this case the "population" would be all 41 nations that participated in TIMSS. A later study conducted an analysis. Sure enough, 8 of the top 10 scoring countries had centralized educational systems. But so did 9 of the 10 lowest scoring countries (Atkin & Black, 1997).

School people are particularly vulnerable to the base rates problem because their normal frame of reference is a sample—their school or their district—not the population at large.

Also related to the causality-from-correlation issue is what we might call "the pump handle criterion." During a cholera epidemic in England, a physician named John Snow noticed that those who got sick all lived near a certain public water pump. People who lived far away did not become ill.

Snow had the pump handle removed and the disease receded. The pump handle criterion is this: Your explanation must include the afflicted and exclude the well. Explanations failing the pump handle criterion abounded in the Jonesboro and Columbine killings. *South Park, Natural Born Killers,* violent television and movies, the decline of the family, the alienation produced by suburban living, the absence of school prayer, the availability of guns, especially guns in the South, and so on were all invoked as explanations of the youths' terrifying and deadly behavior.

The problem is, one of the youths had spent most of his life in rural Minnesota and another in a small town in upstate New York. Most teenagers, even most "Goths" and fans of "Industrial Rock" do not pick up guns and kill their peers. There is no pump handle to be found.

CHAPTER 8

Be Aware of Whether the Statistics Being Used Are Numbers or Rates (Percentages)

Raw numbers often paint a very different picture of a situation than rates or percentages.

The January 9, 1999, edition of the *Washington Post* carried a story under the headline "Immigrants' Ranks Tripled in 29 Years" (Escobar, 1999). There was nothing inaccurate about the headline. The text of the story was accompanied by a table that, to the reporter's chagrin, presented these numbers:

Foreign Borns (in Millions)

1930	14.3
1940	11.7
1950	10.4
1960	9.7
1980	14.1
1990	19.8
1998	26.3

The reporter was chagrined because he had provided the graphics department with another table that wasn't used (Gabriel Escobar, personal communication, January 15, 1999). Taken alone, the figures above make it seem like the nation is being flooded with immigrants. Such a table could provide evidence for those who say we have to stiffen our immigration laws and slow the flow of immigrants into the country.

But the figures given above are *numbers.* We get a different picture if we examine the table that wasn't used, a table showing immigrants as a *percentage* of the population:

1930	11.6
1940	8.8
1950	6.9
1960	5.4
1970	4.8
1980	6.2
1990	7.9
1998	9.8

Clearly, immigrants have been arriving in greater numbers since they dropped to their perigee of 4.8% of the population in 1970, but they still make up a smaller proportion of the population than they did in 1930. If we go back beyond the earliest year presented by the story, we find an even larger proportion of immigrants:

1900	13.6
1910	14.7
1920	13.2

We have often in the past been more of a "nation of immigrants" than currently. The Republic seems to have survived.

A similar phenomenon is heard these days in discussions of job creation and job growth. "The fastest growing occupations are all high tech, high skill." No one has said it in just those words, but the reader has no doubt heard or seen something quite similar. Actual studies of job growth present a more complicated picture. It would be more accurate to say that *some* of the fastest growing occupations required highly skilled workers and some require high-tech skills and some require both. Others do not. The fastest growing occupations, as presented by the Bureau of Labor Statistics in the November 1997 issue of the *Monthly Labor Review* are shown in Table 8.1.

When we use a phrase like "fastest growing," we are speaking of a rate or a percentage. If I make a dollar today and two dollars tomorrow and four dollars the next day, my rate of increase is 100%,

TABLE 8.1   Ten Fastest Growing Occupations

Occupation	In Thousands		
	1996	2006	Q
Database administrators	212	461	1
Computer engineers	216	451	1
Systems analysts	506	1,025	1
Home care aides	202	374	4
Therapy aides	84	151	4
Home health aides	495	873	4
Medical assistants	225	391	3
Desktop publishing specialists	30	53	2
Physical therapists	115	196	1
Occupational therapy assistants	16	26	3
Total	2,101	4,007	

NOTE: Q = Quartile of salary for occupation. "1" is the top quartile, "4" is the lowest.

but in terms of the *number* of dollars, I have earned barely enough for a fast food meal.

Similarly, with jobs, the occupations with the largest numbers of jobs are mostly quite different from those that are growing rapidly. The occupations with the largest numbers of jobs are shown in Table 8.2.

Only the occupation of software engineer manages to make both categories. Many of the occupations with big numbers are low-skilled, low-paying jobs, and it is these that are being most created. If you listen to the radio and catch the monthly unemployment report, you will usually hear it as a good-news/bad-news presentation. The good news is that many jobs were created. The bad news is that the manufacturing sector lost jobs and the service sector made up for it. It is Wal-Mart (the nation's largest retail employer) and McDonald's who are hiring.

A COROLLARY: Ask if the percentage increase really means anything. Beware of words like *double, triple,* or any rate statements without numbers attached to them. In the first "Bracey Report" (Bracey, 1991b), I noted that the number of Advanced Placement (AP) tests had soared from 90,000 in 1978 to 324,000 in 1990. I

TABLE 8.2   Ten Occupations With Largest Job Growth 1996-2006

Occupation	In Thousands		
	1996	2006	Q
Retail sales	4,072	4,481	3
Executives	3,210	4,481	1
Cashiers	3,146	3,677	4
Office clerks	3,111	3,326	3
Truck drivers	2,719	3,123	2
Marketing and sales supervisors	2,316	2,562	2
Nurses	1,971	2,382	1
Waiters	1,957	2,163	4
Food counter	1,720	1,963	4
Clerical supervisors	1,369	1,630	2
Repairers, general utility	1,362	1,608	2
Total	26,953	31,396	

NOTE: Q = Quartile of salary for occupation. "1" is the top quartile, "4" is the lowest.

went on to say that "these changes cannot be explained simply by citing increases in the number of high-scoring Asian students taking the tests. While the percentage of Asians taking AP tests tripled from 1978 to 1990, the percentage of blacks doubled and the percentage of Hispanics quadrupled."

Some years later, a sharp-eyed reader wrote to advise me that she thought it made a difference what the figures doubled, tripled, or quadrupled to. Suppose the proportion of black AP takers doubled from 1% to 2%, that of Hispanics quadrupled from 1% to 4%, while that of Asian AP testtakers tripled from 12% to 36%. That would produce quite a different result than if the proportion of blacks doubled from 5% to 10%, that of Hispanics quadrupled from 4% to 12% and that of Asians tripled from 4% to 12%. In the first instance, a lot of the increase might well be due to the increase in Asian kids, while in the second, it would not (in fact, the reality was somewhere in between the hypothetical examples. The proportion of Asians tripled from 4% to 12%, blacks doubled from 2% to 4%, and Hispanics quadrupled from 1.5% to 6%).

CHAPTER 9

Know Whether You're
Dealing With Ranks or Scores

In a nation obsessed with being number 1, we often see data expressed as ranks. The first national goal adopted at the 1989 Charlottesville summit of President Bush and the governors was to be number 1 in math and science by the year 2000. Of course, depending on how number 1 was defined, we either were number 1 and had been for a long time or hadn't a prayer of attaining that rank. This aspect of definitions is considered more fully in Chapter 11, "Ask How the Variable Is Defined."

For the moment, the important thing to know is that ranks obscure performance. From ranks alone, you know nothing about performance. When they run the hundred-meter dash in the Olympics, someone *must* rank last. He is still the eighth fastest human being on the planet that day and probably not known to the other runners as "Pokey." You don't know what anyone's performance is nor can you know how tightly bunched or spread out the runners were. Maybe all eight in the final heat broke the old world record or maybe no one did. As we saw in Chapter 1, "Beware of Averages," this dispersion can itself say important things in the area of educational research.

The ranks most commonly seen in education and education research are the percentile ranks of scores (stanines, or normal curve equivalents [NCEs] might be used as well, but the percentile rank is the most common; in fact, the NCE is another rank, just a virtually uninterpretable one). Percentile ranks typically compare a given child or group of children (in a school or district) to the performance of a national norming sample. It tells the students, parents, teachers, and administrators how well these children did in comparison to that national norming sample.[1]

Since it is a rank, a percentile rank says nothing about performance. Given that a child brought home a report saying that she ranked at the 75th percentile in mathematics, we can't know how well she did. We know only that she did better than 75% of the kids in the national sample. If the critics of American education are right, then doing better than 75% of our badly lagging kids is nothing to be happy about (the critics' stance is a wee bit overstated).

On the other hand, if the student is doing better than 75% of some elite, this is cause for celebration. Scoring at the 75th percentile on the Graduate Record Exam, for example, means that the student is doing better than three fourths of the norming sample of college graduates. Even if the person scores at only the 5th percentile, the reference group is still a national sample of college graduates, a status attained currently by only about 30% of the population.

If a group contains many members and those members are ranked, it is possible that small differences in scores will make large differences in ranks. For example in the TIMSS (Third International Math and Science Study) eighth-grade science test, American students got 58% correct, just barely above the international average of 56% correct for all 41 participating nations. This score gave U.S. students a rank of 17th place. Had they but gotten 62% correct, just 4% more, they would have jumped all the way to a tie for fourth place. Had they lagged back at 54% correct, just 4% fewer, they would have fallen all the way to 28th place.

NOTE

1. It is possible to have other comparative groups using some kind of "local norms." Big cities often compare themselves against other big cities because they look better in this like-against-like comparison. Suburbs almost never compare themselves against other suburbs because they would not fare as well in like-against-like as they do against national norming samples that include both the urban and rural poor.

CHAPTER 10

Make Sure the Statistic
Used Is the Right One

I mentioned early on that statistics are human creations in need of human interpretation in order to be meaningful. Similarly, the constructs we use to talk about education concepts can be interpreted in different ways. This can get confusing when different concepts use the same word. The notion of "intelligence" meant very different things to Spearman, who thought a single factor, g, controlled most human behavior, than to Thurstone, who thought intelligence consisted of many independent factors. And neither conception of intelligence fits well with the multiple intelligences theory of Howard Gardner.

It is easy to see how people might differ in their notions about intelligence. Unfortunately, there are terms used in education statistics that appear at first sight to have unique meanings but that, on closer examination, turn out to admit of multiple definitions. We must choose which definition we think is most meaningful.

For example, it is often said that America spends more money on its schools than any other nation in the world. This is not true nor has it ever been by any definition. But there are several ways to define how much money nations spend on their schools.

One way of defining money spent is in terms of how much money per student per year a nation spends. Using this definition, of course, requires some considerable manipulation of moneys. As goods and services do not cost as much in, say, Storm Lake, Iowa, as in, say, midtown Manhattan, neither do they cost the same in Spain or in Switzerland as here. In addition, in a world of floating currencies, the "amount spent" can change over even a short period of time. I took a dinner cruise on the Seine, then wrote up the experience for the *Washington Post* without changing the amount. When the article appeared some 4 months after the event, the *Post* editors had recalculated my cost based on currency changes, and the cost of the cruise had dropped almost 10%.

The Organization for Economic Cooperation and Development (OECD) has attempted to correct for such fluctuations and cost-of-goods differences with something it calls Purchasing Power Parities (PPP). If these things work, then we should be able to specify how much the same amount of, say, the same basket of groceries would cost in different countries.

My attempts to get a fix on the accuracy of PPPs have not been successful. But I note here that using PPPs and converting every currency into dollars, OECD's *Education at a Glance* shows that the United States is second in the world among 26 nations in spending for its elementary schools and third in the world for secondary schools. This is as close as the United States ever comes to being number 1 in spending.

Other researchers, including those at OECD, have analyzed school spending in terms of the investment a nation makes in its schools. One study calculated expenditures as a percentage of income. In that case, the United States finished 14th of 16 industrialized nations (Rasell & Mishel, 1990).

OECD's index of school expenditures as an investment analyzes spending in terms of percentage of gross domestic product (GDP) and as a percentage of per capita gross domestic product. In terms of outcomes, it makes virtually no difference which index is used, but it could. Luxembourg, for instance, has a tiny GDP and the United States has a huge one. Luxembourg might need to spend more of its small-sized GDP than we do.

If one calculates spending as a function of *per capita* GDP, though, one removes the impact of different sized GDPs. In all instances, we are talking about spending in terms of how much a single person produces per hour. Using per capita GDP (and overall GDP as well), the United States is smack in the middle of the 19 nations for which the statistic is available.

In a similar vein, a Canadian newspaper article in early 1998 ran under the headline, "Why are boys dumber than girls?" (Killian,

1998). Of course, this headline carries the presumption that boys *are* dumber than girls. How can you know? What is the right statistic?

The author of the story used mostly grades and provincial examination scores along with some ancillary evidence, such as dropping out and the presence of behavior problems. He presented his conclusion as universal: Boys are dumber than girls. Most of his data were anecdotal, though, and limited to Canada, England, and Australia.

Grades, of course, reflect more than smarts. Attendance, demeanor, and completion of home work on time are other factors that can enter into grades. Some teachers reward effort and some punish students who don't work up to what the teacher perceives as their ability. One might be—should be—tempted to find more objective indices. I was asked to comment on this article at a meeting in Vancouver, British Columbia, and merely pointed out that the conclusion was contradicted by the TIMSS (Third International Math and Science Study) scores of Canadian boys and girls. There were only small differences at grades 4 and 8. The differences were larger in the final year math-science literacy test, but at least some of these differences were accounted for by the fact that boys were more likely to be still taking science courses when the test was administered. Elementary and middle school results are presented below.

TIMSS Results, Canada, by Gender

	Percentage Correct	
	Boys	*Girls*
4-math	48	46
4-science	64	63
8-math	59	59
8-science	60	58

Canadian girls did outscore Canadian boys in the most recent international study of reading, something that was true for virtually every one of the 31 countries participating.

The Canadian example might be considered amusing and minor, but the problem afflicts some major policy issues here in the United States. Take class size for example.

The most outspoken doubter concerning class size has been Eric A. Hanushek, an economist at the University of Rochester. Hanushek's statements not only drive home the need to know that the statistic is the right one, but the need to watch for writings that substitute variables that are not really substitutable. Let's clarify that murky statement with a Hanushek (1999) quote:

> While acknowledging the uncertainties inherent in the analysis of nonexperimental data, the striking aspect of the combined evidence on class size is the consistency with which it points to no systematic effects of class size reductions within the relevant policy range. . . . One undeniable feature of 20th-century U.S. schools has been the steady decline in pupil-teacher ratios. The increases in teacher intensity over the past three decades have been much larger than most current policy proposals to reduce class size. (p. 144)

Did the reader notice the sleight of hand? Hanushek starts by talking about "class size," then transitions to "pupil-teacher ratio" without missing a beat or indicating to the reader that he is now talking about something else. Hanushek has been arguing for about 20 years now that "class size" doesn't matter. But his data come largely from changes in pupil-teacher ratio. Pupil-teacher ratio is not the appropriate statistic with which to discuss class size. And Jeremy Finn and Charles Achilles (1999) pointed out that in many schools with the lowest pupil-teacher ratios, students are cramped into overcrowded classrooms.

Hanushek is right to say that that ratio has fallen substantially. It is currently about 17:1. However, average class size, according to the *Digest of Education Statistics,* is about 22 students in elementary classrooms and 25 in secondary classrooms (U.S. Department of Education, 1998).

The difference occurs because the pupil-teacher ratio includes everyone who has a teaching certificate, whether or not they have classroom duties. It includes special education teachers who typically have quite small classes. And, as recent studies have found, a large portion of new money spent on education since 1969 has been spent on special education. The figure would also include teachers of children with limited English, who occur in small classes and whose numbers have been increasing.

Hanushek throughout his papers often writes "class size" when he should be writing "pupil-teacher ratio." The results of experimental reductions in class size and the controversies generated are dealt with in Part II in Chapter 23.

CHAPTER 11

Ask How the Variable
Is Defined

Closely related to making sure the statistic is the right one is determining how a variable is defined. I mentioned this briefly in the ranks versus scores principle, but it deserves more extensive coverage. Too often we find ourselves talking about some educational outcome without thinking about our definition.

If we say that a state or a district is number 1 in reading, we tend to think that reading is reading is reading. But it is not. And different tests define reading differently and measure different skills in different ways. The reading skills tested by the ITBS (Iowa Tests of Basic Skills) are not the same as the skills tested by the Degrees of Reading Power, which is not the same as the NAEP (National Assessment of Educational Progress) assessment, which is not the same as the skills tested by the National Adult Literacy Survey.

In 1991, *NEA Today* put Indianapolis's Key School on the cover with the question, "Is this the best elementary school in the country?" A lot of people would say "probably" and a lot more would say, "If not the best, certainly one of the best." How is *best* defined in this instance? Certainly not in test scores. When Indiana imposed a test-oriented accountability system, Key School faculty worried that they might have to abandon what they considered good pedagogy to stave off the threat of losing accreditation (they solved their dilemma by making drill-oriented worksheets and cajoling parents into doing them with their kids at home. Scores went up so much that the state sent over an inspector to see if they had cheated).

The Key School is based primarily on Howard Gardner's theory of multiple intelligences. To develop each of the seven intelligences, children get a regular curriculum plus a lot of extras. Everyone learns to play a musical instrument and everyone learns a foreign language. There are daily lessons in art. There are lots of activities to foster self-awareness and awareness of others.

The Key school also incorporates Mihaily Czikszentmihaily's notion of flow, as well as a lot of good common sense. For instance, each Wednesday, after lunch, the faculty gather for a planning and evaluation meeting. The students are placed in the charge of parent volunteers and go to the auditorium for a presentation by some group from the community (e.g., once when I was visiting it was a quartet from the Indianapolis Symphony, another time nurses and paramedics). The community group explains what they do, what kinds of skills are needed, what kind of education is required.

The teachers also teach "pods," which involve instruction in some interest that the teacher pursues outside of school—Victorian architecture, pottery making, and so on. The theory is that teaching about things that genuinely interest the teacher is likely to genuinely interest the students. My limited experience suggests it works: A field trip through some Victorian homes in Indianapolis was as well behaved, attentive, and enthusiastic as I've ever seen.

It is a very full day and everyone goes home tired. But the body language of the students says that they are happy to be there. Perhaps the best definition of *best* came from the students themselves. Initially, the Key School was prekindergarten through grade 6. It wasn't long, though, before graduates started sending feedback that they were "dying" in a regular middle school, and the Key School was expanded.

CHAPTER 12

Ask How the Variable Is Defined— And Then Ask What the Criterion Measure Is

Knowing how a variable is defined is only the first half of a two-part process. Once we know that, we have to ask how the criterion or outcome measures are defined (in the 1930s, the process was reduced to a single step by using "operational definitions"; a variable is defined by the operations used to measure it. Not much is made of operational definitions these days.). This part of the question assumed significance when the programs of the Great Society were begun in the 1960s. Up to that point, social programs had been evaluated principally by looking at how much money they had and what they did with it. Now a new question was asked: What happened?

Educators who took federal money for some kind of innovation or reform were now asked to demonstrate that their change had produced some improvement. In many instances, appropriate measures were not readily available and had to be developed. In more instances, program evaluators unthinkingly applied a standardized test to measure program effect.

One needs to ensure that there is a match between the variable of interest and the criterion measure that is used to detect changes in that variable. If one developed a program to increase what Robert

Sternberg calls Practical Intelligence, one would not want to measure it by changes in a norm-referenced achievement test. Those tests have nothing to do with the application of intelligence in a practical setting.

Similarly, if one were looking to improve students' self-esteem as learners, one would not be advised to use a measure of global self-esteem. Such a measure would incorporate too many other self-esteem factors besides self-esteem as a learner. One could hypothesize that changes in self-esteem as a learner could result in improved learning over time and to use scholarly and global self-esteem measures in sequence. Actually, one would be well advised to steer clear of self-esteem: It's a slippery concept with highly fallible measures.

CHAPTER 13

Differentiate Practical
and Statistical Significance

Few concepts have caused as much confusion in education as the concept of "significance." Researchers almost invariably mean statistical significance, while practitioners often think they mean practical significance. Findings that are statistically significant might have zero practical import. Findings that are not statistically significant might be vitally important. From a test of statistical significance alone, you can't tell.

People often present findings in terms of statistical significance, then argue that the group or program—whichever had the higher score—is the better treatment. This is an error. Statistical significance is silent about program treatment.

Let us suppose that for students having difficulty learning to read you install the remedial program, Success for All, in one school and maintain your regular reading program in another, appropriately matched school (which we will hereafter call the "control group," although it is not a control group in the usual sense. A control group receives either no treatment or a placebo. Control groups in educational research typically receive the ongoing treatment— the standard curriculum). At the end of the year, the students in Success for All have higher reading scores on average than those in the control group. The difference is statistically significant. Does this mean that Success for All is an improvement over your regular reading program and should be adopted by the district? Maybe, maybe not.

A test for statistical significance is only a statement of odds, not of program impact. You found a difference in the average reading scores for the two groups. A test of statistical significance tells you only how likely it is that a difference of that magnitude could have occurred by chance. Or, as statisticians like to say, if the two samples had been drawn from the same populations or populations with the same mean.

Tests of significance are necessary in the first place only because we don't test whole populations, we test samples, and we usually test samples of convenience, which is to say, the kids in the nearby schools. Any time you do not test the whole population, there is some chance that your sample is not representative. Now, if you test everyone in the district and the district is the only universe of interest, then there is no point in running a test of significance: The difference is real no matter how large or small it might be.[1]

Tests of significance were defined for relatively small samples, groups of say 25 to 40 people. The tests are affected by sample size. The larger the sample, the greater the chances of finding significant differences. With a very large sample, virtually any difference will be significant.

Even with a large sample and highly significant results, significance remains a statement of odds. As such, there is *some* chance that if you judge that the difference between the groups is real, you will be wrong. Different levels of significance adjust your chances. The most lax standard of significance in educational research is the .05 level. If you listen to researchers, you will hear them speak in a peculiar tongue about significance; about a result that is significant at the .05 level they say, "pee is less than point oh five." This means that the probability (represented by the letter p) of the differences occurring by chance is less than 5 times in 100.

If you accept the .05 level as your standard, you will be right 95 times out of 100, but you run a risk that 5 times out of 100 or 1 time in 20 you will be wrong. The .01 level reduces the risk to 1 time in a hundred and .001 to 1 time in a thousand. Judgment is called for, and it matters how important the call is. To me the idea of building a scientific edifice on results that have a 1 in 20 chance of being wrong seems risky. I go for $p = < .01$ or better.

Of course, if the results are *replicated* by other research, your confidence grows that the results are real. Replication is de rigueur in the natural sciences. A fact is not a fact until it has been observed by a variety of researchers. When two researchers in Utah claimed to have accomplished cold fusion, laboratories all over the world sprang into action to try to replicate the results. This was an unusually fast spurt of activity because the import of the findings was so great—we would no longer need to burn fossil fuels for energy—but less dramatic results also get replicated.

Alas, replication counts for little in educational research, meaning that you can't get promotions and tenure for it. Actually, it is held in even less esteem. Every so often, some faculty member at some university proposes that the researches for master's theses should be replications of some important-seeming but singular study. The proposal is invariably shot down, usually in the name of developing independent thinking.

There are a variety of ways to get beyond statistical significance. One is to cast the results in terms of a relatively new statistic called Effect Size or ES. In its simplest form, an ES is calculated by subtracting the mean score of the control group from the mean score of the experimental group and dividing by the standard deviation of the control group (some researchers favor using a pooled standard deviation formed of both experimental control groups).

The formula for effect size is as follows:

$$ES = \frac{X_e - X_c}{\sigma_c} \qquad 13.1$$

Note: ES = Effect Size; $\overline{X}_e$ = mean of experimental group; $\overline{X}_c$ = mean of control group; and σ_c = standard deviation of control group.

The ES shows the impact of a treatment in terms of standard deviations. An ES of +1.00 would represent the equivalent of one standard deviation; this means that the treatment would move a student at the 50th percentile before the treatment all the way to the 84th percentile (in a bell-shaped distribution, 34% of all scores are between the mean and +1.00 standard deviations, and another 50% are below the mean).

Effect sizes as large as +1.00 are seldom seen. Most researchers feel that an effect size of between +.20 and +.30 begins to take on practical significance, but even this is a judgment call. A treatment that produced an annual effect size of +.33 for African American students would wipe out the black-white test score gap in 3 years. A treatment yielding an effect size of only +.20 would take 5 years, an outcome that many would still judge very worthwhile.

There is also a matter of cost. Success for All, a popular program for at-risk students, is not a cheap program. There might be others that yield similar results for less.

There is also a matter of importance. James Shaver gives the example of a device that costs $510, takes 17 hours to install on a car, and increases average mileage from 16 to 16.68 miles per gallon. If the variability of miles per gallon was 1.00, this would yield an ES of .68. Would you buy the device?

Shaver thinks most wouldn't, since it takes so long to install and would take so long to pay for itself.

But what if a new medical procedure cost $510, required 17 one-hour visits to the doctor, and increased life expectancy by an effect size of .68, from, say, 70 to 76.8 years? Lines outside the doctor's office would be long. (Shaver's two-part series on statistical significance, set as a conversation between two teachers, is highly recommended for further understanding of significance, chance and effect size; see Shaver, 1985a, 1985b).

A program that produced a given impact on reading scores might be considered worth acquiring, but not a program that produced the same effect size in geography scores. This conclusion is not intended to make geographers mad. It is simply based on the assumption that reading is a skill that has implications for all curriculum subject areas whereas knowledge of geography does not.

The treatment also needs to be evaluated in terms of its impact on students and teachers. During my stint as a teaching assistant for Psychology 1 courses at Stanford, some professors assigned a programmed textbook written by B. F. Skinner and a colleague. "Read this book," the professor would say, "and I guarantee that you will have mastered Skinnerian theory." He could have also said that he guaranteed that the students would hate Skinnerian psychology and programmed textbooks. Reading programmed texts is simultaneously boring and frustrating. A program that raised reading scores but left students with a bad feeling about reading might not be the program you want to institute.

If a program or treatment comes to you with an evaluation cast only in terms of statistical significance, you will likely want to gather collateral evidence about the effectiveness of the program.

NOTE

1. For the sake of convenience we are assuming that our tests are perfect measures, containing no measurement error.

14

Look for Trends,
Not Snapshots

Given the prevalence of nostalgia and given the prevalence of know-nothing-kid comments and the prevalence of the general feeling that schools are underachieving, it is not surprising that people are prone to give negative interpretations of snapshot data (*snapshot* is a lay term for what researchers call cross-sectional data, data taken at only one point in time). Given the prevalence of nostalgia, they are also prone to set unreasonably high standards.

For example, the State Board of Education in Virginia decided to impose a new curriculum on the state and to develop tests that would measure the extent to which schools met the standards. The tests, by all accounts, are good ones. They have good content validity—that is, they measure what they say they measure. They also have high reliabilities.

So far, so good. The State Board also convened groups of teachers and administrators to set the passing scores for the tests. So far, so better. But the Board then ignored the recommendations of its cut-score setting committees. The procedure for judging cut-offs presents a range of possibilities, and the recommendation is to go with some point in the middle of the range. The Board ignored this recommendation and set scores at the upper extreme. In some instances, the Board placed a cut score above any of the recommended scores.

The result has been a disaster. When the first test results—the first snapshot—arrived, it was found that 98% of Virginia's schools had failed to meet the Board's passing score.

Is it reasonable that 98% of Virginia's schools should lose their accreditation—the consequence if passing scores are not forthcoming? Here's an international perspective on the reasonableness of the situation:

In the Third International Math and Science Study (TIMSS), 41 nations participated at the eighth-grade level.

When the TIMSS-NAEP (National Assessment of Educational Progress) linking study was conducted by ETS (Educational Testing Service), it was found that 6 nations outscored the state of Iowa in math and only 1 of the 41 countries outscored Iowa in science.

Students in Iowa score between the 62nd and 68th percentile on achievement tests.[1]

In Fairfax County, Virginia (and other places; I just happen to live in Fairfax County), students score between the 64th and 83rd percentiles, with most scores being in the upper 70s.

Thus the data sequence is: Iowa's students outscore virtually the whole world, and students in Fairfax County, Virginia, trounce students in Iowa. Yet only 6% of the 202 Fairfax schools passed the tests.

Some dismissed these results saying that since they didn't "count," no one took them seriously. Ultimately, schools that fail lose accreditation and kids who fail can't graduate, but it was true that accreditation did not hang in the balance on the first round, nor were the results entered on students' permanent records. After the results though, newspaper stories abounded with how the various districts were working to improve. And editorials abounded, mostly blaming the schools, not the tests, for the results. If nothing else, the results from the first administration were the two-by-four that got the donkey's attention.

Yet, after a year of intense practice, only 22% of Fairfax schools passed the second round. Statewide, 93% were still failing.

It is much more reasonable to use any kind of snapshot as the baseline of data and to chart progress from that baseline. As the Minimum Competency Testing craze was moving through the nation in the late 1970s, Gene Glass, then at the University of Colorado, pointed out that educators have a hard time specifying how much of something is "good." It is easier to specify that more of something is better (Glass, 1978).

If we have 20% of our students taking Advanced Placement (AP) courses, 25% is better. If we are at the 60th percentile on a test, 63rd is better. If 74% of our students go to 4-year colleges, 78% is better.

Maybe. Even making something better is not without its trade-offs. What if we increase the number of students in AP courses to a point where some of them experience frustration? What if people cheat to raise test scores? What if we end up sending to college students who would be better off in some technical or vocational program?

In connection with AP courses and tests, *Washington Post* writer Jay Mathews (1999a) found that some districts discouraged kids from taking AP courses or, if they let them in the courses, discouraged them from taking the tests, so that the district's average score would look good.

It is for these reasons and others that Richard Rothstein of the Economic Policy Institute has proposed that a school or district establish an accountability system that specifies *all* of the outcomes that the district values (Rothstein, 1999). The district then weights the indicators in terms of importance and combines them to create a composite index. The system is then judged on changes in the composite—progress—not on the component parts. In the current madness to look only at test scores, this will not be an easy system to establish, but it is a wise one.

The system that Rothstein created for the Los Angeles Unified School District included not only student outcome variables, but "process variables" such as student and staff attendance rate, graduation rate, on-time graduation rate, violent incidents, amount of graffiti present, proportion of air-conditioned classrooms, adequacy of restrooms, percentage of on-time safe bus trips, and a lot of other variables that people value for themselves.

Already, with the focus only on test scores, we have had an assistant superintendent in Austin indicted. We have had a principal in Virginia resign. We have stories about students in Massachusetts getting the questions early and one being arrested for refusal to take the test. Reports say that up to 95% of students in some Michigan districts are refusing to take the tests. In Chicago, a teacher was fired for publishing test questions. When accountability looks only at the snapshot of a single outcome, strange things happen.

NOTE

1. As a digression, we can note that one operational definition of an otherwise slippery concept, "world class," could be the 65th percentile on achievement tests. If Iowa kids average around the 65th percentile, and if Iowa outscores 85% of all nations in math and 96% of all nations in science, then the 65th percentile seems like a reasonable definition of "world class."

CHAPTER 15

Beware of Trends

Doesn't this contradict the last principle? No, because what you need to beware of is believing that a trend will continue at the same rate it has in the past. If a company sells one million widgets in year 1 and two million in year 2 and four million in year 3, we have a trend in which the number of widgets sold is doubling every year. Can it go on like this? Well, if we assume only a domestic widget market and that widgets last 10 years, then in year 6 of the trend there will be 125,000,000 widget owners, or roughly one in every two Americans. Not many products are this successful.

Similarly, a 10% gain in test scores from the 45th percentile would take a school almost to the national norm. But each ensuing 10% gain requires a larger increase in terms of the number of percentile ranks required for a 10% gain. And the trend is likely to end when the test is changed.

That is, suppose a district is administering an achievement test and looking to gain X% or Y percentile ranks each year. As long as the district uses that one test, all ranks are referenced to the year that the test was last normed. But tests get renormed. If other districts have been improving since the earlier norming year, the same raw score that yielded satisfactory progress to date will conform to a lower, maybe a much lower, percentile rank. Recall, the 50th percentile is determined by the median raw score. If everyone has been improving, that median will be moving up.

CHAPTER 16

Ask What the Consequences Are Even If the Interpretation of the Data Is True

This principle sounds awkward formulated in the abstract, so let's consider it in the concrete. When the TIMSS Final Year Report appeared, people howled:

> "American high school seniors have scored far below their peers from many other countries on a rigorous new international exam in math and science." (*Washington Post*) (Sanchez, 1998, p. A1)

> "American high school seniors—even the best and brightest among them—score well below the average for their peers participating in TIMSS." (*Education Week*) (Viadero, 1998)

And so on.

One can appropriately criticize the media for being so uncritical in accepting these results as being from a "rigorous new international exam." One can criticize even more the notion that the American 12th graders were comparable to the students in other countries. As shown in Part III, they were not "peers." The systems are not comparable.

Ignore all of these objections for a moment. An appropriate and nonsarcastic response to all of these laments is, "So what?"

If American seniors *are* far behind their peers in other countries, does it matter? In what ways? What are the consequences? Can we find any?

In the case of TIMSS, it is not easy to find data to get alarmed about. For instance, while other economies are either stagnant or in crisis, the United States is enjoying the greatest sustained economic expansion ever. We have a surfeit of mathematicians and scientists. We greatly outpublish scientists from other nations in the scientific journals, even taking into account the size of the country. We have a virtual lock on Nobel Prizes. We could and should ask if scientific courses of study are proportionately available to females and minorities as they are to white males. We could ask if our students know enough science to make them good citizens in a technologically complex society where discussions are rampant about global warming and the ethics of cloning (we could also ask if the educated layman can ever know enough to make decisions about these complicated issues). We could ask if students are learning enough science and math to get the good jobs in the new technologies.

There are lots of questions that can be asked. Some will be answered yes, some no. But it should not be the case that we assume that the test scores themselves tell us what is good and bad about the system. We have reached a point where test scores have assumed an importance they do not deserve. And we might be losing sight of some important outcomes of our educational system that could be lost in a race for ever higher test scores.

A tale from Karel van Wolferen's 1989 book *The Enigma of Japanese Power* seems appropriate here. Van Wolferen reports the case of a Japanese scientist who won a Nobel prize. This scientist, however, had not lived in Japan for many years. He obtained a bachelor's degree at the University of Kyoto, but came to the United States for his PhD from the University of California at San Diego. He worked for a while in Switzerland, then settled in at MIT, where he conducted his award-winning research.

Van Wolferen reported that opinion in Japan was universal: Had the scientist remained in that country, he would never have won. In part, the rigid bureaucracy would have held him back. In part, the press for consensus, so overwhelming in Japan, would have prevented him from taking high-risk research strategies that often run down blind alleys but sometimes terminate in Nobel prizes.

Before we alter the system to produce Japanese-style test scores, we had best lay out all of the things we value in the way that Rothstein does and decide which of those might be at risk if we decide to emphasize test scores more.

Consider what the Japanese media are saying about the Japanese system:

> The Japanese educational system has already become obsolete and useless for the development of society. Primary and middle school education must be changed into a decentralized system with more options. High school education must have more freedom and must be more competitive.
>
> The failures:
>
> First, the current educational system fails to enhance the student's spirit of independence. Few young people head for a foreign country and compete with top-level people there. . . . Individuals must have an independent mind to choose, participate and act on their own, without being constrained by the government or companies, and take responsibility for what they have done.
>
> Second, the educational system is ineffective in developing students' ability to think for themselves. If there is the need for innovation in economy, science, technology, culture, and other fields, creativity holds the key to Japan's future. In the current system, which focuses on the "average" student, it is difficult to encourage originality, creativity, and an adventurous spirit. ("Education Reform Is Key," p. A15)

The paper goes on at some length with its litany of failures, but you get the picture. Given my skepticism about American media, I might be prone to discount this description of Japanese failures, but it is corroborated by what both Japanese reformed and outside observers report as well.

Consider this from an American teaching in Japan:

> There is one important effect of Japan's education system that is not addressed: the incredible stunting of the students' social and psychological development. My students have all the emotional maturity of American elementary school students. If I ask a girl a question, often she will sink to the floor in embarrassment at being asked to answer a question. These are

19-year-old high school seniors I'm talking about. The boys aren't so dramatic; they just pretend the teacher doesn't exist if they are unsure about things. Socially, these students are almost incapable of doing anything on their own. . . . I close with this comment: I consider the Japanese schools to be a national, institutionalized system of child abuse. (Boylan, personal communication, April 30, 1993)

Clearly, this person's sole referent is the Japanese high school. Japanese elementary and middle schools are much more pleasant places to be, but all of these comments do suggest that Japan is paying a considerable price for its high test scores.

In 1987, the National Academy of Education observed that many of

those personal qualities that we hold dear—resilience and courage in the face of stress, a sense of craft in our work, a commitment to justice and caring in our social relationships, a dedication to advancing the public good in our communal life—are exceedingly difficult to assess. And so, unfortunately, we are apt to measure what we can, and eventually come to value what is measured over what is left unmeasured. The shift is subtle, and occurs gradually. (Glaser, 1987, pp. 51-52)

Given the current madness about testing, the shift has occurred, but not subtly.

More consideration is given to the diversity of outcomes we ought to be looking at in the opening of Part II.

CHAPTER 17

Beware of
Changing Demographics

In talking about the dangers of nostalgia, I mentioned Arthur Bestor's lament that 50 years before his 1953 book, half of all high school students took Latin or Greek while in Bestor's day only a quarter of the students studied any language at all. Bestor's nostalgia was in part misbegotten because of a sea change in demographics, namely an enormous increase in the holding power of high school. In 1903 only a tiny proportion of the age-eligible population bothered with high school, while in 1953 the country was rapidly moving toward universal secondary education.

I used to tell audiences in Iowa that they were critical to an understanding of educational trends in this nation because they were frozen in time. About the only way their demographics had changed was the addition of television to homes. They remained 98% white, agricultural, with no large cities. We could thus give ready interpretations to test score trends in Iowa. We are losing this capacity as Iowa now has large pockets of Cambodians, Mexicans, and Bosnians who do not speak English as their native tongue.

A look at trends in test scores over time in, say, California would not be very meaningful. During the Great Depression, many impoverished farmers from the Midwest made their way to California. Later, as California became known as the Golden State, many people seeking not only a living but upward mobility flooded the state. When the gold dulled, flocks of Californians made their way back to

Arizona, New Mexico, Nevada, Utah, and Colorado. As a result of recent waves of immigration, at the end of 1999, half of all students in California were Hispanic. Looking at trendlines for test scores in California would be an exercise in frustration—we wouldn't know what variables were producing what changes.

There are smaller perturbations that affect our ability to interpret educational trends. For instance, the eastern part of a Virginia county I once lived in was not as affluent as the western part. It had lower test scores. Not too long ago a high-tech firm announced it was putting a major facility into the eastern part of the county. Test scores will rise as the well-educated people who come to work at this facility bring children who tend to do well on standardized tests. This will initially have nothing to do with the quality of the schools.

Later, the quality of the schools might have an impact on the future quality of schools: Well-educated parents tend to be more demanding of their schools and might cause the superintendent and principals to seek out more effective teachers or to implement a more demanding curriculum.

In fact, it is very difficult to know much about education changes with certainty. For example, today's parents are much better educated than their parents, and since test scores are related to educational levels, test scores ought to be higher. On the other hand, in the past a higher proportion of students dropped out, taking their low test scores with them. If the schools today have greater holding power, all other variables being equal, test scores ought to be lower.

Richard Rothstein (1998) penned a small booklet on this problem, *The Way We Were?: Myths & Realities of America's Student Achievement*. He begins by noting the dangers of nostalgia, but also noting that even if our memories were not distorted, our experiences would be difficult to relate to today's schools:

We can't control our interpretation of experience for relevant background factors and selection bias. In our youth, many of us (along with most public school critics) attended stable, middle-class public schools. Within those schools we were tracked into college-bound curricula. It is these experiences that we compare to the "inferior" academic performance of today's students— not only today's students who are in comparable schools, for they, we may be forced to acknowledge, are as well educated as we were. Instead, we compare our own relatively homogeneous, even segregated school experiences to the experiences of children whose counterparts in earlier generations either dropped out of school or were tracked into nonacademic programs. (p. 25)

Demographic shifts have greatly distorted changes in NAEP trends. Looking at the overall averages, one sees only modest gains. These gains mask larger gains by different ethnic groups. This is discussed in full in Chapter 25 on "falling" test scores.

CHAPTER 18

Try to "See Through" Graphs

Sometimes a picture is worse than a 1,000 words.

Graphs can be deceiving. Sometimes the deception is deliberate, sometimes it is innocent—the grapher altered the scale in order to get the whole graph on a single sheet of paper, for instance. Or, in at least one instance, the same graph was presented on different sized paper. Figures 18.1 and 18.2 show the SAT decline over time. The first graph is from an article by Charles Murray and Richard Herrnstein (1992) in *The Public Interest,* a physically small journal. The second is from the original version of *Perspectives on Education in America,* better known to many as the Sandia Report[1] (Carson, Huelskamp, & Woodall, 1993).

The bottom two curves from the Sandia Report present the same information as the *Public Interest* article. However, the Sandia Report used regular, letter-sized paper. In addition, the Sandia engineers wanted to present the data not only for the two sections of the SAT, but for the two sections combined (the uppermost curve). They thus used a scale that ran from 400 to 1,000, in contrast to the Murray and Herrnstein chart, which goes only from 400 to 500. The same SAT fall looks a lot scarier when compressed into the narrow Murray and Herrnstein scale.

Distortion of meaning often occurs in the presentation of test score charts, as in Figures 18.3 and 18.4. These figures present the same information. Figure 18.3 begins at the 50th percentile, truncating half of the whole scale. When the entire scale is shown

Figure 18.1. Decline in SAT Scores, Graphed on a 100-Point Axis

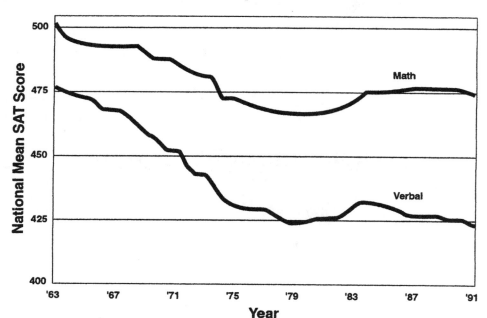

SOURCE: Reprinted with permission from *The Public Interest,* No. 6 (Winter 1992), p. 33. © 1999 by National Affairs, Inc.

Figure 18.2. Decline in SAT Scores, Graphed on a 600-Point Axis

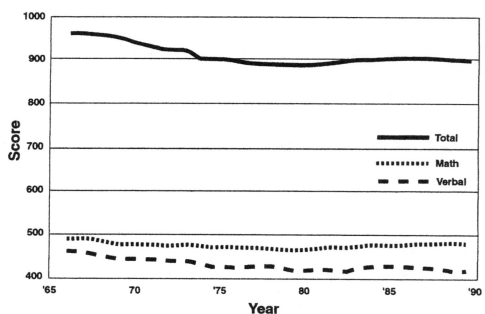

SOURCE: C. C. Carson, R. M. Huelskamp, & T. D. Woodall. (1992). *Perspectives on Education in America. Journal of Educational Research, 86,* 259-310.

Figure 18.3. Bar Graph in Which Differences Between Two Schools Appear Large, Due to Omission of the First 50 Points of the Scale

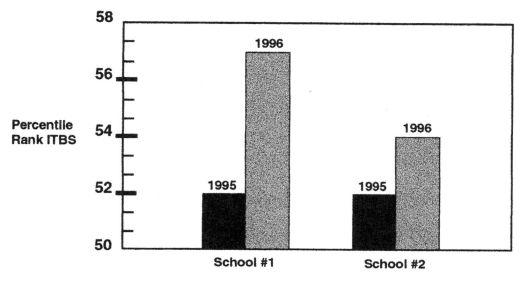

Figure 18.4. Corrected Bar Graph in Which Full Range of Points for Given Ranking Are Supplied

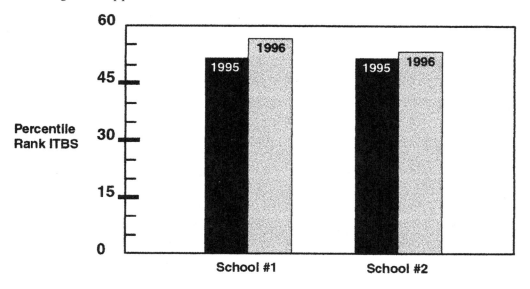

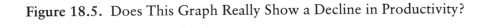

Figure 18.5. Does This Graph Really Show a Decline in Productivity?

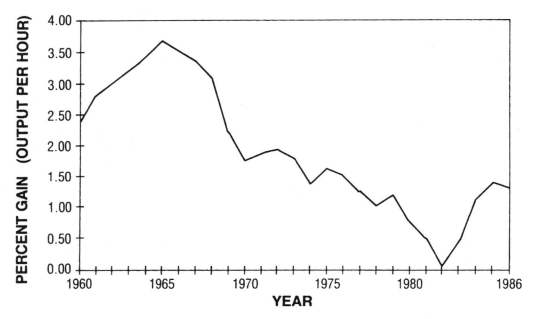

SOURCE: William B. Johnson and Arnold H. Packer. (1987). *Workforce 2000: Work and Workers for the Twenty-First Century.* Indianapolis, IN: Hudson Institute, p. 38. Used with permission.

(Figure 18.4), the gains from Time 1 to Time 2 appear much less impressive.

Finally, take care to determine that the graph actually presents what it says it presents. Figure 18.5 is taken from *Workforce 2000,* a 1988 publication of the Hudson Institute (Johnson & Packer, 1988). The legend says that, "Productivity has declined substantially since 1965." The label on the vertical axis, however, says "Percent Gain." Percentage gain is a measure of how much productivity has improved. Productivity did not fall. Productivity gains slowed. We got more productive more slowly from 1965 to 1980, but at no time did productivity fall. For productivity itself to have fallen, the curve would have to dip below zero on the vertical scale, which it never does.

A matter of fact: Studies have consistently found the American worker to be the most productive in the world. From 1995 to 1997, productivity grew at about 2% a year, and in 1998 it grew by reporter wrote, "Many experts think growth in the range of 2% is probably as good as it gets in the current economy." The writer noted that many now feel that the great expansions of the economy and productivity were themselves aberrations produced by the end of World War II (yet in the fourth quarter of 1999, the economy grew at a 5% rate!).

NOTE

1. This report, compiled largely in 1990 and suppressed by the political appointees of the Bush Department of Education, appeared in print as the entirety of the May/June 1993 issue of the *Journal of Education Research*.

CHAPTER 19

Beware of Big
(Small) Numbers

Large numbers can be just that—large numbers—and they can indicate significant changes. For instance, in 1978, 98,000 Advanced Placement (AP) tests were taken. Twenty years later, the number had grown tenfold.

But large numbers can also be used to impress and/or intimidate. My local National Public Radio (NPR) radio station is partly underwritten by Virginia Power, the state electricity utility. The blurb for Virginia Power notes that its employees have donated more than 1,000,000 hours of community service in the past decade. That looks like a lot. It works out to about 10 hours per employee per year. This is in no way meant to denigrate the community work of Virginia Power employees. The country would be better if more companies had such programs. It is only to show that what look like large numbers in the aggregate might look somewhat different when presented on a "per capita" basis.

The reverse is also true, of course. Small numbers can have large effects in the aggregate. A 2% increase in productivity is a significant gain in the context of America's seven trillion dollar economy.

CHAPTER 20

Beware of Generalizations

Someone once said that no generalizations are worth a damn, including this one. This principle could be rephrased as beware of "overgeneralized" data or "romanticized" data. Or, beware of cliches, which often consist of generalizations. Data from educational research is usually complicated. Human behavior is multiply determined; that is, many forces can operate synergistically to produce an outcome, or they can work antagonistically. See the discussion on the effects of reducing class size in Chapter 23 under "Class Size." When someone speaks in broad generalizations about data from research, chances are they are romanticizing and oversimplifying the actual findings.

Thus from TIMSS, emerged the cliche, "The American math curriculum is a mile wide and an inch deep." If this is true, how come the students in Illinois's 20-district First in the World Consortium did so well? At some ages they *were* as good as the top nation, Singapore. How come a cluster of states scored better than all but 6 of the 41 nations participating in TIMSS? And how come some scored better than only 3 of the 41? Obviously, in some places, kids are learning as much as they are in the highest-scoring countries. And in some places they are not learning much at all—only Colombia, Kuwait, and South Africa underperformed them. First world, third world, all right here at home. If the cliche were true, such variability wouldn't exist.

Similarly, one section in *The Learning Gap* is headlined "The American Emphasis on Ability" (Stevenson & Stigler, 1992, p. 96) and another is labeled "The Asian Emphasis on Effort" (p. 98). The data underlying these sections have been overgeneralized to the cliche, "Americans believe in ability, Asians believe in effort." For example, Harvard's Katherine Merseth (1993), writing in *Phi Delta Kappan,* stated baldly that "effort receives little credit for contributing to successful learning in mathematics—or, for that matter, in any subject" (p. 549)

The data are not so clean and, in this case, *The Learning Gap's* authors, Harold W. Stevenson and James W. Stigler, have misinterpreted their own data. Their survey data do reveal that American mothers and American children do think that ability is more important than Asian mothers and Asian children.

But . . . and it is a big but, American mothers think effort is almost as important as Asian mothers, and American kids think that effort is just as important as Asian kids do. The situation is much more complicated than the cliche would let you think (the data appear on pages 101 and 102 of *The Learning Gap*).

It is often useful to follow up this principle with an earlier one, "Show me the data."

PART II

Aspects of
Achievement

In 1980, at the height of the minimum competency testing madness, I didn't think the country could get any more test crazy. I was wrong. We seem to be heading toward an era in which virtually every aspect of education is evaluated with tests. Moreover, there has been a retreat from the development of performance-type measures that would broaden the number of educational outcomes measures.

We also have forgotten some very important words written by the National Academy of Education, cited earlier, but worth repeating:

> [Many of] those personal qualities that we hold dear—resilience and courage in the face of stress, a sense of craft in our work, a commitment to justice and caring in our social relationships, a dedication to advancing the public good in our communal life—are exceedingly difficult to assess. And so, unfortunately, we are apt to measure what we can, and eventually come to value what is measured over what is left unmeasured. The shift is subtle, and occurs gradually. (Glaser, 1987, pp. 51-52)

The shift has occurred. There is no longer anything subtle about it.

The retreat from performance-oriented tests back to the factoid-oriented, multiple choice variety could end up being a total debacle for education. I say this based partly on my own convictions about what testing can and cannot do, and based as well on the experience of others, both formal and informal.

Here's a true story. When I was a graduate student, I spent a year in Hong Kong and was invited on occasion to lecture on developmental psychology to advanced undergraduates. When I showed up the first time, I came as a product of my culture. In this case, that meant preparing a lecture, but also some questions to stimulate thought and discussion. I was getting my doctorate in psychology and so had not encountered the common phrase in education, "wait-time." I had had some clinical training though, and knew that therapists should not jump in and talk when a client was silent. I asked my first question. The students sat there. I stood there. They sat there. They won. I went on with my lecture.

The scene was repeated several times. Afterwards, I asked the head of the psychology department, who had been present during my trial, "What happened?" He grinned and said, "Oh, they were probably embarrassed that you didn't know the answers."

Well, it has now been more than 30 years since this experience, and I wondered if it were still a condition of education in the Orient. I had occasion to ask a professor of education in Taiwan, and he replied, "Yes, professors' questions are often met with stony silence." Teachers are purveyors of information, not stimulators of thought.

The kids in Hong Kong do very well on standardized tests. This is itself quite a success story (assuming for the moment that the students from Hong Kong in TIMSS [Third International Math and Science Study] comprised a representative sample). When I lived there, teaching was primitive to say the least, especially for students dwelling in the "Resettlement Estates"—slums created to handle the massive influx of refugees from the People's Republic of China. Education mostly consisted of reciting material aloud in unison. Yet if you believe, as I do, that thinking is a use-it-or-lose-it skill, these students are being deprived of important educational experiences.

The kids in Japan do very well on standardized tests, better than the kids in Hong Kong. But another story indicates that this performance, too, has consequences of some import. The demographer Harold Hodgkinson visited Japan for the first time in 1997. He returned with many interesting observations, including a story about an episode at a soiree. Hodgkinson was approached by a man who asked, "Why don't Japanese win Nobel prizes?" Hodgkinson considered for a few moments whether he wanted to answer this question at all and finally said, "To win Nobel Prizes, you must do original research and invent things." The man wrote it down. Hodgkinson's story corroborates an earlier one told by van Wolferen in *The Enigma of Japanese Power* (recounted in this book in Chapter 16).

I have been told often that Westerners simply can't fully appreciate the degree to which Japanese fear being wrong. Nobel prizes are all about being wrong. The path toward one requires the personalized approach to research that on occasion sends a scientist to Scandinavia to collect a bundle. A friend once lived next to James Watson in the days before he and Francis Crick won the Nobel prize for figuring out the structure of DNA. Watson once passed her in an agitated state, waving a paper, and said, "Linus doesn't have his Nobel yet!" "Linus" was Linus Pauling, Watson's chief rival in the race to crack the code, and the paper Watson was carrying described Pauling's latest failure.

In the previous section, we noted some of the failures of Japanese education as described by Japanese media. Similar sentiments have been expressed by the Minister of Education in Singapore, the highest test-scoring country in the world. They were expressed during a tour of the United States to see how he might get his kids to be more like ours.

So, there is a clear downside to tests.

It is also true that our educational system looks to prepare people for a much more fluid social structure, and that is an important aspect of achievement. Even the military in this country adopted a slogan, "Be all you can be." I can't imagine this slogan existing elsewhere. The outcomes of the system are noticed abroad. I once spent a breakfast listening to a German industrialist (at the next table) railing about the archaic German corporate culture. He described how the president of a company arrived in his chauffeured Mercedes while the vice president drove his own Opel. I might have discounted this perspective as reflecting only one person's views, but a few days later on NPR's *All Things Considered,* another German observer declared that if Bill Gates were German, he'd still be stuck in middle management.

The restricted vision that comes from looking at education through the eyes of test scores makes it more important, then, to step back and look at the nature of testing and to examine aspects of achievement that are important but that, in many instances, are not test based. Absence of graffiti is a school achievement in some places and a critically important one. Attendance rates of both staff and students count, too.

I recommend that at some time the reader watch the Annenberg/ PBS series *Minds of Our Own*. As the first tape begins, an interviewer thrusts a battery, a bulb, and a wire into the hands of various students and asks them if they can make the bulb light. Most of them say no. One even says it can't be done. This might not be disturbing in eighth graders before they have been exposed to a high school science curriculum. But these students wear caps and gowns. They are preparing to graduate from MIT and Harvard. I talked with the producer of this series, querying him about how representative these students were. He replied that a substantial proportion of those interviewed failed to make the bulb light.

The video then cuts to middle school students who are asked if they were put in a room with no light, could they see an apple, even if they couldn't make out its color. They all aver they can, once their eyes adjust. They are then put into a light-free space for some time, and they are never able to see the apple. They emerge convinced, though, that had they been given enough time, eventually they would have come to see the fruit.

Finally (for this exposition; the video has other examples), we return to the bulb, battery, and wire problem with high school students who have just completed a segment on electricity in an honors physics class with a teacher who is described as very successful. One of the "best" students, as measured with paper-and-pencil tests, fails to make the bulb light. This surprises and appalls the teacher. Most surprising, the student makes the same mistakes she made before the teacher provided instruction.

Given some directed hands-on experience, the students come to understand how to make the bulb light. The teacher resolves to use a hands-on performance-assessment teaching strategy. This is remarkable, given that the guy has enough experience to retire if he thought the change to be too wrenching. He is aware, however, that not everyone will approve of the change. He declares that some people will say, "You just spent five class periods teaching them about batteries? You should be able to cover that in 15 minutes!" (Information about how to locate these videos is provided in Chapter 23 under "Adequacy of Scientific Laboratory and Field Equipment").

*   *   *

In the remaining exposition, we will briefly examine the history of testing and the basic structure of the most common forms of tests: norm-referenced, criterion-referenced, and performance. We will look at their various strengths and weaknesses. We will also take a look at one of the most famous (notorious?) tests, the SAT, and at an increasingly visible test, the National Assessment of Educational Progress (NAEP). Readers interested in a more extended discussion of tests and their uses are referred to my booklet, *Put to the Test: An Educator's and Consumer's Guide to Standardized Tests* (Bracey, 1998a).

CHAPTER 21

The Rise of Testing

It is only in recent years that large numbers of people have started paying attention to tests. In 1960, say, few states had state testing programs. The National Assessment of Educational Progress (NAEP) did not exist. Since there were more students who wanted to go to college than there were seats in college classrooms, teachers, counselors, and admissions officers paid attention to the Scholastic Aptitude Test (SAT). The media and the public did not. It would be another 3 years before the SAT would start its 20-year decline. Students might have fretted about the SAT, but they were not supposed to see their actual scores (my principal told me only that my results would get me into most colleges, but carefully arranged the report form so that I could peer across the desk and see the actual numbers).

In 1960, Banesh Hoffman was 3 years away from writing *The Tyranny of Testing*. Hoffman's book was a bit misnamed because it mainly lamented the tyranny of multiple-choice tests, which Hoffman felt often penalized the exquisitely analytical mind that could argue for two or more of the choices. Two years earlier, a minimum competency test for high school graduation had come into existence in Denver, Colorado, but it would be another 15 to 20 years before these tests started popping up all over the country. No international comparisons allowed us to compare our students with those in other nations. The few international studies that did exist looked at curricula, not test scores.

In 1960 we "knew" our schools were inferior to those of other nations because in 1957 the Russians had launched Sputnik, the first manmade satellite, and that "proved it." But test-based evaluations of schools were still in the future. I recall taking the "Iowas" each year and then sitting around, in the upper grades anyway, chatting with teachers about what the results meant.

It's not that tests weren't around. In 1900, the College Entrance Examination Board decided it needed to bring some coherence to high school curricula and decided further that the best way to do that was with a series of essay examinations in the various curriculum subject areas. During World War I the multiple-choice format was invented, which made mass testing easy and cheap. These tests were used to try to determine who would make a good tank driver, who a good gunnery officer, and who could make it as a soldier only on the front. The sole interest in testing was to make discriminations among different people. The College Board, impressed with the advances in such testing, decided to abandon its cumbersome essay system of almost 20 tests and use a combination of essay and multiple choice questions in a single test to see if it could predict who would make a good college student and who would not. In 1926, it developed a new test it called the Scholastic Aptitude Test. Its principal developer, Carl Campbell Brigham, called it a "mere supplement" to the rest of the high school record and urged that people not invest much importance in it. IQ tests had taken shape in 1918 when Lewis Terman had improved on Binet's invention, and taken their modern form with Terman's 1937 revision of the test he called not the Terman-Binet, but the Stanford-Binet after the university that housed him.

As regards the use of tests in schools, there is at least one unfortunate aspect of the history of testing: Tests were developed by people who had little or no interest in what went on in classrooms. As noted, virtually the sole use of tests was to create different scores for different people so other people could make differential predictions from those scores (if everyone scores the same, no predictions are possible). As the technology of scoring made it ever more economical to use multiple-choice format questions, that format came to dominate (tyrannize, Hoffman would say) the testing arena. The psychometricians (as testing people call themselves) were quite satisfied with this format and, as a consequence, experimentation with other test formats dwindled to virtually nothing.

The disconnect between teaching and testing became important as the American public began to lose confidence in its schools.

Criticism of schools has always been abundant, but the frequency and intensity of criticisms increased soon after World War II. Writing in 1989, education historian Lawrence Cremin noted that between 1950 and 1985 the proportion of Americans with high school diplomas had more than doubled, from 34% to 74%, while the proportion with college degrees had more than tripled, from 6% to 19%. Access had expanded, the curriculum had expanded, and public control of the schools had expanded. "Yet [this expansion of schooling] seemed to bring with it a pervasive sense of failure. The question would have to be 'Why?'" (Cremin, 1989).

That indeed would have to be the question, and different people have answered it differently. Historian Henry Perkinson (1991) claims that people knew that schools were not the best, but "on the whole, the schools did a fairly good job of selecting and training youths for their future careers. However, by the Fifties, many realized that fairly good was not good enough" (p. 151).

The criticism does reach record levels in the fifties, but I disagree with Perkinson's interpretation of why. People were certainly *afraid* that the schools were not good enough, and this fear was cast in terms of the catastrophic consequences that would befall the globe should the Cold War ever heat up. Admiral Hyman Rickover, the father of America's nuclear Navy, cautioned repeatedly, "Let us never forget that there can be no second place in a contest with Russia and that there will be no second chance if we lose." Against the Red Menace, the schools were the earliest line of defense. It was from their ranks that we had to produce the mathematicians, engineers, scientists, and even foreign language speakers we needed to prevent world domination by communism (Rickover, 1958).

Along with the tensions of the Cold War, the fifties saw a rise of nostalgia for some earlier golden age of American education. In contrast to Perkinson's contention, Americans were no longer seeing their schools as "fairly good," they were now remembering a time when they were better. Recall that the subtitle of Arthur Bestor's influential 1953 book, *Educational Wastelands,* was *The Retreat* From Learning in Our Public Schools (emphasis added).

When a basketball-sized satellite called Sputnik soared into orbit in October 1957, the fears about the Russians and the longing for a better, earlier time collided to produce a profound wave of anxiety. "Crisis in Education" said the red letters on the March 24, 1958, issue of *Life.* The story inside, the first in a five-part series, compared the lackadaisical American school system to the rigorous, intense system of the Soviet Union as it followed two high school ju-niors through their school week. The Russian student does complex experiments in science and reads from *Sister Carrie*. The American walks his girlfriend home, practices for a school musical, and, re-treating from a geometry problem on the blackboard, "amuses his classmates with wisecracks about his ineptitude." Clearly the nation is in trouble.

Life gave two full pages to novelist Sloan Wilson,[1] who pulled no punches:

> The facts of the school crisis are all out and in plain sight—and pretty dreadful to look at. First of all, it has been shown that a surprisingly small percentage of high school students is study-ing what used to be considered basic subjects. . . . People are complaining that the diploma has been devalued to the point of meaninglessness. . . . It would be difficult to deny that few di-plomas stand for a fixed level of accomplishment, or that great numbers of students fail to pursue their studies with vigor. . . . It is hard to deny that America's schools, which were supposed to reflect one of history's noblest dreams and to cultivate the na-tion's youthful minds, have degenerated into a system for cod-dling and entertaining the mediocre. (Wilson, 1958, pp. 31-32)

Nostalgia strikes: The system has "degenerated." And one can al-most feel Wilson toying with a next sentence: "Our nation is threat-ened with a rising tide of mediocrity." That sentence, though, would have to wait 25 years and take its place among the opening rhetori-cal flourishes of *A Nation at Risk* (National Commission on Excel-lence in Education, 1983).

A brief digression. I located the American student. He became an airforce pilot and is currently a commercial pilot. Despite consid-erable effort on the part of National Public Radio reporter Anne Garrels, and her staff in Moscow, I have no evidence that the Rus-sian ever existed. As Garrels pointed out, the Moscow school was presented as typical and there was no way that an American journal-ist and camera crew would have been permitted entrance to such in 1957. Garrels did not rule out fabrication on the part of *Life* editors. More likely, she felt, was the possibility that the story had been a re-ward to the boy's father for some kind of exceptional service to the Communist Party.

Schools never got over Sputnik. When, 12 years later, the United States landed a man on the moon, something the Russians tried to do and failed, to the best of my knowledge no one knelt before a statue of Horace Mann and said, "Thank you for this wonderful educational system."

There were, in addition, more shocks along the way. In 1970, Charles Silberman's *Crisis in the Classroom* appeared and received a great deal of attention.

Silberman's tome was, at the very least, curiously named, as Silberman himself observed. In the opening chapter, Silberman took note of the fact that the Educational Testing Service (ETS) had reviewed 186 instances in which the same test had been administered to students at different points in time. In 176 of them, the difference favored the more recent point in time. Silberman claimed that overall the studies showed a general improvement of about 20%. So where was the crisis?

The crisis lay not so much in the schools as academic institutions, but as social institutions. The schools were one of many such institutions that were not delivering everything they ought to be. Silberman asked, "Why are the schools so bad?" They are so bad, he answered, because they are obsessed with order and control:

> Because adults take schools so much for granted, they fail to appreciate what grim, joyless places most American schools are, how oppressive and petty are the rules by which they're governed, how intellectually sterile and aesthetically barren, what an appalling lack of civility obtains on the part of teachers and principals, what contempt they consciously display for children as children.
>
> [Carleton Washburn said] "every child has the right to live fully and naturally as a child. Every child has the right also to be prepared adequately for later effective living as an adult." In the grim, repressive, joyless places most schools now are, children are denied both rights. (Silberman, 1970, p. 116)

Silberman (1970, chap. 6) offered not only a critique, but a solution, "The Case of the New English Primary Schools." Journalist Joseph Featherstone (1967a, 1967b, 1967c) had recently limned a three-part description of these schools in *The New Republic*. Schools were being created in England that seemed to honor Washburn's dictum. Indeed, one report sounded like a paraphrase of Washburn:

"Children need to be themselves, to live with other children and with grownups, to learn from their environment, to enjoy the present, to get ready for the future, to create and to love, to learn to face adversity, to behave responsibly, in a word, to be human beings."

Ironically, the introduction of this reform, the English "open education," might have made things worse in the long term. Open education swept through large parts of the United States where the English concept quickly got confused with open space. Walls came down. Children sat around in small groups. I don't know when the backlash started, but when I left the country in mid-1973, people were talking about open education, Piaget, and integrated projects. When I returned in late 1976, the talk was all "Back to Basics." When I landed a job as Director of Research, Evaluation and Testing for the Virginia Department of Education, my first task was to design a set of very traditional tests to measure very traditional educational outcomes. It was called The Basic Learning Skills Testing Program.

The next year, a panel convened by the College Board to look at the then 14-year decline of SAT scores released its report (College Board, 1977). The panel saw the fall as the complex interaction of many factors, most of them outside of schools. The media and the public saw a falling line that looked like a children's playground slide. To them, the line simply meant that the schools were failing.

Thus, various events, books, and commission reports sustained the sense of crisis created by Sputnik. When he became secretary of education in 1981, Terrel Bell set about looking for what he called in his memoir, "a Sputnik-like event" to focus people's attention and energies on education (Bell, 1988). Lacking one, he more or less half-heartedly created the National Commission on Excellence in Education. It produced what many called "the paper Sputnik," *A Nation at Risk.*

Risk opened with colorful, cold-warrior rhetoric (the commission had hired a professional writer), claiming not only that we were threatened by a rising tide of mediocrity, but that if an unfriendly foreign power had imposed this mediocre system on us, "we might well have considered it an act of war."

Risk was a hit. In the month following its publication, the *Washington Post* carried no fewer than 28 articles about it. No one hinted at any skepticism about the report's findings (it is, in fact, a golden treasury of slanted, selected, and spun statistics). The only hint of criticism came from the *Post's* resident curmudgeon, James J.

Kilpatrick. Kilpatrick (1983) observed that there was nothing new in the report's findings. Looking back at other critiques, Kilpatrick declared that

> they all said the same things, and they all made basically the same recommendations. They said the quality of education in our public schools is shamefully low. . . . These recommendations are sound. They have been sound for the last 30 years. . . . Why hasn't anything been done about all these years of similar findings and recommendations. The cause, at bottom, is that the American people don't give a damn about their public schools. (p. A19)

New York Times columnist Russell Baker limited his critique to an analysis of the rhetoric. Examining "a rising tide of mediocrity," Baker declared that "a sentence like that wouldn't be worth more than a C in tenth-grade English. I'm giving them an A+ in mediocrity" (Baker, 1983, p. A23).

Education organizations accepted the report for the wrong reason—they thought it would be a stimulus to increase spending. Since we have all these terrible problems, surely the money must be forthcoming to fix them. Wrote AASA (American Association of School Administrators) Executive Director, Paul B. Salmon (1983),

> AASA welcomes the Commission's report. We are pleased that education is back on the American agenda. We know that recently school administrators have been frustrated by state lids on taxes, cutbacks in federal funds, and White House support for tuition tax credits, but we believe that this report can be an important first step in redefining and reexamining our national commitment to education. (p. 1)

Risk did not address tuition tax credits. In fact, it addressed none of the Reagan education agenda, causing a great schism in the White House about whether or not Reagan should accept the report. Ed Meese and the conservatives lined up on one side; Jim Baker and Mike Deaver led the charge of the moderates and prevailed. *Risk's* message, reduced to a single word, was "more": more courses, more rigorous courses, more time in class, more time on task, a longer day, a longer year, better trained teachers, higher salaries.

But the impact of *Risk* was to raise America's anxieties about the schools to new levels, and shortly after *Risk* appeared, "more" morphed into "different." At first, discussion about "different" was cast in terms of "restructuring" the public schools. Soon, though, more and more discussion was heard about "alternatives" to public schools—charters, vouchers, private management, and so on.

The effect of *Risk* was indeed to throw the spotlight on the schools, but it left people asking if it was *possible* to reform the schools and, even if it was possible, was it worth the effort. Maybe it was better to close up shop and create a new institution.

Obviously, in such an atmosphere, any claims of success by educators were bound to be suspect. Educators' words could not be trusted. They were being "defensive." Or they were only speaking what it was "in their self-interest" to say.

Tests, on the other hand, lay in a realm outside of the educators' defenses.

Tests were constructed by organizations devoted to that purpose. Tests did not give slippery qualitative information, but precise-looking numbers, like scaled scores and percentile ranks. America is a normative nation. We want to know who is number 1 and where we (or our kids) are in comparison. Tests are designed precisely for that purpose.

It was also true that in the years between Sputnik and *A Nation at Risk* the uses of testing had expanded beyond the role of "The Great Sorting Machine." While people were still principally looking at tests as sorters—who should be in gifted and talented, who will do well in college, who should be in the academic track and who the vocational—people had also found other purposes for testing.

We pause to take a brief look at these other purposes, but first we issue a great cautionary note: A test that is designed for one purpose and accomplishes that purpose well might be inappropriate for other purposes. This problem is recognized in the *Standards for Test Use* jointly adopted by the American Educational Research Association (AERA), the American Psychological Association (APA), and the National Council for Measurement in Education (NCME) (American Educational Research Association, American Psychological Association, and the National Council on Measurement in Education, 1985).

Despite the warning, such inappropriate use of tests occurs quite often. For example, the state of North Carolina constructed a statewide curriculum, then developed tests to determine the extent to which the curriculum had been put into place. Such tests examined district performance. Once the tests were in place, however, some districts began to use the results to make decisions about promotion and retention of individual students. Ignoring the fact that retention in general is bad practice, tests designed for use with large systems do not have the requisite precision for making decisions about individuals.

MONITORING

Tests are sometimes used by parents, teachers, and others to corroborate other information. This use has increased as people have been concerned about "grade inflation" or about teachers cutting deals with kids that give a student a passing grade if the student doesn't disrupt the class, or yielding to pressure from parents who fear that less than an "A" will lower the odds of their child getting into the right college. This use of tests in part is the game of "Who Do You Trust?" If the two sources of information give conflicting results, which one do you put your faith in? The test is "objective" (but it can be taught to). The teacher has had a much more extensive opportunity to observe the child's performance under many more circumstances (but might be subject to parental pressures to give a good grade). There is also the question of whether or not the test and teacher assessments measure the same "thing." A fact-oriented history test might not fit well with a teacher who is stressing a historical understanding of trends and why historical events unfolded the way they did.

DIAGNOSIS

Most tests in use today have extremely limited utility in rendering a diagnosis of a particular problem a child is having. On achievement tests, for instance, there are too few items in any skill area to give much of an idea, and the areas themselves are too broad. The most noticeable exception to this occurs in mathematics, where tests can indicate if a child is having difficulty with something such as place value or converting fractions to decimals. Even here it is important to determine if the test matches instruction. In the post-Sputnik era, it became fashionable to teach mathematics via set theory, and tests, responsive to curricular changes, incorporated the language and concepts of set theory. Today's children, even those acing today's tests, would perform poorly on these tests because they would not know set theory terminology.

There are tests designed to diagnose specific conditions that might warrant placement in special education, but these are not the tests in common use. The usual norm-referenced, commercial achievement tests are probably best thought of in a medical analogy. They are thermometers. They can indicate when a situation departs from normal, but *cannot* provide information about what to do next. A thermometer cannot provide a prescription.

Once, when states were surveyed about the purposes of the state programs, the most common response was "educational improvement." But this is what most tests cannot lead to because there is no direct link to what shows up on a test score report and teaching.

PROGRAM EVALUATION

Since the 1960s, tests have been invoked to determine whether or not innovations, programs, or reforms have had any impact. There are often risks associated with unthinkingly using a test to look for changes in desired outcomes. The tests might or might not match well what the intended outcomes really are. These risks are described in Principles 11 and 12 (Chapters 11 and 12, respectively), and we need not repeat that discussion here.

TEACHER (PRINCIPAL, SUPERINTENDENT, BOARD) ACCOUNTABILITY

This is the current growth industry of testing, even though a look at a *Washington Post* article some 13 years ago indicates the issues and the arguments were rife and rampant then, too. People must be held accountable! Despite the superficial reasonableness of this position, there are a number of problems with it. First, is the test an appropriate criterion? This, at the very least, is subject to debate. If one teacher teaches material that appears on the test while another teaches other equally valid material, other things being equal, the first teacher will likely look better on the test. But what if the second teacher can provide pedagogically sound reasons for approaching the topic the way she did?

Not everything can be taught, but one of the problems in American education is that we try. The curriculum analyses from TIMSS (Third International Mathematics and Science Study) found that American textbooks in math and science are three times as thick as those in other nations. The textbooks here, unlike in other nations, are commercially produced, and since the publishers want to sell to the largest possible market, they include everything. What I have called "the tyranny of scope and sequence" coerces teachers to try to get through it all. The cliché that emerged from TIMSS was that the "American math curriculum is a mile wide and an inch deep." While not wholly accurate by any means, there is enough truth to it to conclude that teachers should teach fewer topics in more depth. But what if different teachers opt for different material, and what if the material of Teacher A is more aligned with the test than that of Teacher B? While it is true that a teacher cannot teach it all, it is even more true that a test, usually 25 to 40 multiple-choice items in length, cannot test it all.

Teacher accountability via tests also collides with a common means of teacher assignment. Good or veteran teachers get the good classes. Poor or new teachers get the tough assignments. Logically, one would think it better educational practice to do the reverse, but that seldom happens. Even if this were not true, students do not arrive at a given grade as blank slates. Should a teacher be held accountable for the previous teacher's neglect, or for the forces outside of school that influence achievement?

Teacher accountability through tests also collides with the law of WYTIWYG (pronounced witty-wig): What You Test Is What You Get. So you'd better be very careful about what you test. The impact of WYTIWYG is especially virulent when tests are the sole instruments of accountability. It is important, therefore, to make tests only one part of your accountability system. We noted in Chapter 14 in Part I an accountability system that spells out all of the outcomes a district values and makes the district work to improve all of them.

As the developer of this system, Richard Rothstein of the Economic Policy Institute observed that people want to look good and if you evaluate them on one thing, they will focus attention on that one thing, perhaps to the detriment of the rest of the system.

Rothstein picked an example from the old Soviet Union. When shoe factories there were held accountable for productivity in making shoes, some of them made only small sizes. They thus made more shoes faster and saved leather at the same time.

We don't have to go outside of education for examples of this force at work. When John Murphy became the superintendent of Prince George's County, Maryland, public schools, one of his goals was to get test scores up and another was to eliminate the black-white score gap. The psychology involved was not exactly benign. Murphy designated his office conference room as the "applied anxiety room." On its wall hung charts showing the test score trends in all of the schools in this very large system.

It "worked." Scores rose. The gap between blacks and whites did not disappear, but it narrowed considerably, and black students were scoring comfortably above the national norm. But with accountability hanging on the slender thread of test scores, that became the focus of at least some teachers and principals. Stories told of how instruction in some schools looked like getting ready for a test. Students would approach the blackboard, read a "stem," and then choose one of four or five preselected answers.

Murphy resisted the advances of several organizations that proposed external program evaluations. Murphy was abetted by the fact that the state of Maryland had used one particular version of a test far too long. Eventually, though, as always happens, the state changed its test. As usually happens, scores fell. They fell all over the state, but in Prince George's they plummeted. Some scores that had been above the national norm fell all the way to the 18th percentile.

By the time of *le deluge,* though, Murphy had taken a job in another state.

A less extreme example of gaming the system comes from Virginia at about the same time. Testing was so important in Virginia, where I was Director of Research, Evaluation and Testing, that we had constructed a computer program to detect unusual patterns of test score changes. One year the computer had spit out the name of a small rural county to which we drove to investigate. The superintendent was new and declared that his students didn't take the tests seriously. They were mostly going to work on their parents' farms or in farm-related industries and few were headed for college.

The superintendent had a problem with his low scores, though: Although his district was rural, it was close enough to several suburban districts to be included with them in the newspaper "box scores" each time the tests results were published. To get his kids to take the tests seriously, he removed the tests from the academic forum and placed them in the athletic arena. The goal was no longer to do well to show how smart you were or how well your teachers had taught you. The goal now was to do well for the same reason that you tried your best in sports: to beat the arch-rival adjacent county.

This too, "worked." If you asked students at the high school what they were going to do on the SRA (the test battery in use at the time), they would respond enthusiastically, "Beat Orange County!" The week of testing, teachers dressed up as cheerleaders and held a pep rally wherein the students in the affected grade were cheered on by their nontested peers. Scores rose between 15 and 30 percentile ranks, depending on age and test.

At one level this is appropriate, since it gives an idea of students performing at their best. On the other hand, the percentile ranks are produced by comparing this district's scores to those of the national norming sample. No one held a pep rally for the national norming sample. Thus the ranks are really not valid because the two groups took the tests under vastly different motivational conditions.

Sometimes people try to avoid the pitfalls discussed above by testing the students of a given teacher twice, once in the fall and again in the spring. This introduces another source of problems: When people know they will be evaluated like this, they behave in ways that depress scores in the fall, enhance them in the spring. Tests are short and it takes only a few items to make a noticeable change. Shaving a couple of minutes off the testing time in the fall and adding a couple in the spring might do it, as might a little pep talk in the spring.

In 1998, the superintendent of Alexandria, Virginia, public schools received a contract with a clause calling for bonuses if test scores rose by a certain amount. I hope he's on good terms with his teachers.

To repeat: People want to look good. If the variable they're being held accountable for is narrowly focused, the curriculum is likely to become narrowly focused, too. And worse. TAAS (Texas Assessment of Academic Skills) scores went up in 1999 and so did the number of students excluded from testing. An assistant superintendent in Austin, Texas, was indicted and fired in 1999 for tampering with TAAS scores (some legislators' reactions to the incident were to propose changes in the law. Currently, such action as alleged against the assistant superintendent is a misdemeanor. These legislators want to make it a felony). A principal in Virginia resigned over similar charges (it is not yet a crime in the Old Dominion), but as this is written in early 2000, legislation is under consideration.

STUDENT ACCOUNTABILITY: PROMOTION, RETENTION, GRADUATION DECISIONS

I imagine we will see some litigation in this arena before everything plays out. There are two likely sources: First, the AERA, APA, NCME *Standards of Test Use* state that no decision should be based on a test alone. Yet, in many states, that is precisely what is happening. Students cannot graduate in Virginia without passing the Standards of Learning Tests. Ohio has its Proficiency Tests, Texas has the Texas Assessment of Academic Skills. And so on. It is only a matter of time—the point at which these tests deny someone a diploma—before these many testing programs become jobs programs for lawyers.

The likely defense from the tests' sponsors will be that the student had many opportunities to take the test. This is likely to be true. Programs that contain the graduation sanction usually offer from four to six opportunities for the student to pass. This substantially reduces the chance that the student is what is known in testing terms as a "false negative." A false negative in this instance would be a student who fails the test but whose skills are actually above the test's cutoff score.

If their achievement is really above the cutoff score, you ask, how come they failed? The answer, in part, is that no test is a perfect measuring device. They all contain what psychometricians call measurement error. The amount of error can be calculated statistically. The chances that the measurement error in the test produced a misleading result drops a great deal as the test is repeated.

The second source of litigation is likely to be the tests' differential impact: More poor and minority students will fail than middle-class white students.

"Social promotion" is currently a favorite scapegoat for people to beat on. President Clinton came out against it. The American Federation of Teachers decried it. The subject even turned up in an article in the British periodical *The Economist.* In terms of retention, the evidence seems clear: In the aggregate, retention in grade does not work. Kids react to it negatively. It increases the probability of dropping out. And it doesn't help academically. The U.S. Department of Education recently issued a "guide" to districts on how to end social promotion. The guide concluded, though, that even for children who get after-school help, or in-school help, or help on weekends, or who go to summer school, retention in grade is not an effective strategy.

Why do people think it works? Largely, I think, because they are not in a position to do a controlled experiment. Retained students usually have difficulty when they repeat the grade, too. They do better the second time around, but not a lot. Teachers and parents, observing a child struggling on material that has already been covered, draw the reasonable, but wrong inference that the child would be experiencing even greater difficulty had he or she been promoted.

However, for a variety of reasons, there have occurred situations in which some children were retained while others of equal achievement were promoted. The promoted children fare better.[2]

The distinction, incidentally, between "social promotion" and promotion based on "merit" is often a false one. Students who are identified as having difficulty are often provided with special programs, with after-school programs, Saturday programs, and summer school. Those who advocate retention are left to explain how a number of countries that practice no retention at all do better in international comparisons than the United States. When I spent a summer in Denmark, I found educators there to consider retention in grade barbaric, something that could be practiced only in a nation that really didn't like its children.

NOTES

1. The choice of Wilson was not as arbitrary as it might at first appear. Wilson had served on several national education commissions and had been the education editor for the *New York Herald Tribune*.

2. The best treatment of the research on promotion and retention is *Flunking Grades* by Lorrie Shepard and Mary Lee Smith. A decade after that book, I wrote a 50-page review of the research literature. It is available for $15. Interested persons may contact me at gbracey@erols.com.

CHAPTER 22

Types of Tests

The tests used in schools are referred to as "standardized tests." They are standardized in many ways: The format is the same for all children, the questions are the same, the time permitted to complete them is the same. To obtain these kinds of standard qualities, tests are most often given in groups. Where tests are given to individuals, as with some IQ tests, the test administrators themselves have been highly standardized through training in how to administer the tests. The qualities seem normal to us now, but well into the 20th century, it was common for students to be assessed individually, with each child receiving a different question. This permitted much error to enter the system, as when a bright student received a particularly difficult question he couldn't handle and a not-so-bright student received an easy question. When Binet first began his work that led to IQ tests, the concept of standardization was largely missing, not only from the procedures to be used, but in how such words as *normal* and *subnormal* were defined.

The most common type of test remains the norm-referenced test, although states are increasingly moving to customized state-level tests that have no norms. These are sometimes called criterion-referenced tests or CRTs but, as will be discussed momentarily, they are not criterion referenced in the original sense of that phrase. They are often referenced to a curriculum or set of standards, but these do not meet the specificity of "criterion referenced" as initially defined.

To construct an NRT (norm-referenced test), the test publisher surveys the commonly used texts and workbook materials, constructs items, and has the items reviewed for "content validity." Content validity addresses the issue of whether or not a test measures what it says it measures. When sufficiently satisfied with the content validity, the tester can move to item try-outs to see if the items "behave properly." Proper behavior in an item is a matter of certain statistical properties. For instance, most questions will be answered correctly by 40% to 60% of the students. Such a success rate maximally disperses the scores of those who take the tests (and, recall, dispersion in order to make differential predictions was the prime goal of tests initially). Questions that are answered correctly by a high proportion of those who have overall low scores, or are missed by students who have overall high scores, will also be tossed aside.

With a set of content valid, properly behaving items, the publisher then administers the test to as many as 200,000 students so chosen that they represent the nation as a whole. The average (median) score on the test, the 50th percentile, is then called the "national norm" and all results are presented in terms of how they compare to this norm, hence the term norm referenced.[1]

The fact that the norm is the 50th percentile, an average, bothers some people. It means that half of all children are always, by definition, below average. This also occurs with most definitions of "grade equivalent"—the score of the average child in a particular grade. There are other ways of defining grade equivalent, but the previous one is the most common.

Norm-referenced tests have traditionally arrived in multiple-choice format, although there has been a trend in recent years to require writing samples and to provide some open-ended mathematics questions where students must calculate the answer and sometimes show their work as well. The multiple-choice format is another quality of tests that bothers some people because it requires the test maker to try to fool the student. Only one of the four or five answers is usually the right answer. But the wrong answers, the "distractors" as they are called, must be sufficiently enticing to lure some of the students to choose them. Otherwise, everyone will get all of the items correct, and we can't make differential predictions or selections or much of anything.

There is another quality of multiple-choice tests that bothers me, and it was captured marvelously 50 years ago in a letter to the editor of *The Times* of London:

Sir:

Among the "odd man out" type of questions which my son had to answer for a school entrance examination was, "Which is the odd one out among cricket, football, billiards, and hockey?"

I say billiards because it is the only one played indoors. A colleague says football because it is the only one in which the ball is not struck with an implement. A neighbor says cricket because in all the other games the object is to put the ball into a net; and my son, with the confidence of nine summers, plumps for hockey "because it is the only one that is a girls' game." Could any of your readers put me out of my misery by stating what is the correct answer, and further enlighten me by explaining how questions of this sort prove anything, especially when the scholar has merely to underline the odd one out without giving a reason?

Perhaps there is a remarkable subtlety in all of this. Is the question designed to test what a child of 9 may or may not know about billiards—proficiency at which may still be regarded as the sign of a misspent youth?

Yours faithfully,

T. C. Batty

Batty has pointed out an important problem. While the various reviews, field tests, and norming procedures would no doubt weed out many questions prepared locally and subject to various interpretations, the fact remains that within the multiple choice format, we have no way of knowing why a student picked a particular answer.[2] It might have been from rote recall. He might have guessed blindly. She might have reasoned her way to the right answer. He might have reasoned his way to the wrong answer. Younger children in particular can often give good rationales for their choice of what adults view as the "wrong" answers. Younger children can also be influenced by personal experience, such as the group of upstate New York young-sters who declared in their test answers that the animal most likely to be found on a farm was a giraffe. A nearby petting zoo called "Ani-mal Farm" used a giraffe as its logo.

Other problems with multiple-choice tests, notably the inability of existing tests to tap higher-order thinking and complex skills, are discussed in Part III, Chapter 32.

CRITERION-REFERENCED TESTS

Instead of referencing scores to a norm, we can reference them to some well-defined set of behaviors and watch an individual's prog-ress over time in reference to those behaviors. Those behaviors are the criteria against which performance is measured, hence the phrase "criterion-referenced testing." This kind of referencing oc-curs in athletic competitions such as diving or ice skating. Judges can be trained—standardized—so that one gets almost perfect agreement about how the performance rates. Occasionally, patriotism or politics slips into the judgment and for this reason the extreme scores at either end are discarded, but in general the agreement among judges is quite remarkable. The theory behind criterion-referenced testing is that achievement of any skill can be specified on a continuum that runs from zero amount of skill to conspicuous excellence.

Alas, the subjects that students study in school and what they ought to be able to do with them are not clearly specifiable the way ice skating is. There are areas like "reading" and "history" that de-scribe large, nebulous curriculum domains, unlike, say, ice skating. Moreover, teachers are often most pleased with a performance when it produces something unexpected. It is when students offer creative but reasonable answers to complicated questions that teachers most see intelligence in operation. Indeed, among the strongest criticisms of writing assessments are the ones claiming that they will stifle creativity and, ironically and paradoxically, good writing. The scorers of the writing assessment have to apply criteria as do diving judges. Essays that go "outside the box" or "push the envelope" or in any way show the kind of creativity teachers love are likely to be punished with lower scores.

What pass for criterion-referenced tests in most places are norm-referenced tests with no norms, just cut scores, scores that students must attain in order to pass the test. They look just like norm-referenced tests and, indeed, norms could be produced. The cut score is a score above which students pass and below which they fail. This is indeed a kind of criterion, but it is not referenced to anything specific.

Cut scores are also arbitrary, which is not necessarily a fatal flaw: *Arbitrary* can relate to arbitration as well as to capriciousness. What we must keep in mind is that there is no technology, no scientific process for setting a cut score that is free of arbitration; we can only hope to keep the capriciousness at bay.

Just as norms could be gathered for what started out as a criterion-referenced test, so criterion-referenced interpretations can be made of norm-referenced tests. This is not a good idea since, as was noted earlier, tests designed for one kind of use might not function well in another setting. Apparently, though, the City of Chicago is using the Iowa Tests of Basic Skills in a criterion-referenced way, retaining in the eighth-grade children who do not attain a certain cut score.

I have earlier noted that all tests come with some measurement error and that multiple testings are often offered to reduce the chance of such error affecting the decision about a person's "true score." Another type of adjustment often occurs in the setting of the cut score itself. The most common measure of error in a test is called the standard error of measurement, and it can be calculated in a straightforward manner. Typically, once a cut score has been established, it is lowered by one, occasionally two, standard errors of measurement to improve the chances that a failing score really is a failing score and not an artifact of measurement error.

PERFORMANCE TESTS

Most people are probably not as interested in an airplane pilot's score on a multiple choice test of navigation as they are in whether he or she can get the plane up, over to its destination, and down safely. As noted in Chapter 32, in at least some settings, performance tests are the only way of determining whether students have really understood the concepts being taught. In other cases, students can learn only by performing. For instance, in the 1960s and 1970s, schools tested for "writing" skills with multiple choice tests. These tests are actually test editing skills—the student reads a sentence, parts of which are underlined and with the numbers 1 through 4 or 1 through 5 at the underlinings. The student has to pick the number where an error in spelling, grammar, or syntax occurs. As a consequence of using this type of test, students did not learn to write. Later, most states added some form of writing assessment.

Despite the earlier-mentioned problems of writing assessments penalizing creativity, the general level of writing has probably improved. When Texas developed a writing assessment, several of the best papers in the entire state were set aside and given to scorers 4 years later. They rated as only average.

The importance of performance testing is seen most clearly in the area of critical or higher-order thinking. Some have argued that multiple-choice questions can tap higher-order skills (Worthen & Spanel, 1991). Those multiple-choice tests that do, however, are typically found in graduate school and contain stems that are sometimes a whole page long. Such a stem allows for the presentation of much information, and the answer choices can then be framed with a great deal of subtlety. This does not occur in commercial achievement tests or even the SAT (this aspect of tests is discussed in Chapter 32).

Indeed, in most testing situations, students who stop to think about their answers are punished for doing so. Commercial achievement tests are typically constructed with a time limit that permits about 90% of the testtakers to finish 90% of the items. Thinking in this kind of situation is not a good testtaking strategy.

The inability of multiple-choice questions to tap higher-order thinking becomes clear when we describe the qualities of such thinking. Lauren Resnick (1989) of the University of Pittsburgh has pointed out that higher-order thinking is difficult to specify simply, but when people talk about it, they usually mention certain qualities:

Higher-order thinking

1. Is nonalgorithmic—that is, the path of action is not fully specified in advance

2. Tends to be complex—the total path is not "visible" (mentally speaking) from any single vantage point

3. Often yields multiple solutions, each with costs and benefits, rather than unique solutions (think about thinking about buying a car or a house)

4. Involves nuanced judgment and interpretation

5. Involves the application of multiple criteria, which sometimes conflict with one another (think about thinking about some problems you face as a schoolteacher or administrator)

6. Often involves uncertainty—not everything that bears on the task at hand is known (think about waging a war in Kosovo without ground troops)

7. Involves self-regulation of the thinking process—we do not recognize higher-order thinking in an individual when someone else "calls the plays" at every step

8. Involves imposing meaning, finding structure in apparent disorder—sometimes the hardest part of solving a problem is figuring out what the problem is; sometimes the nature of the problem does not become specified until *after* a solution has been found

9. Is effortful—there is considerable mental work involved in the kinds of elaborations and judgments required

A student who deploys the above described thinking on a typical test is in trouble. The SAT requires a student to answer 85 verbal questions in 90 minutes and solve 60 math problems in the same amount of time. Not much time available for thinking here. And yet, isn't this what education in a democratic society is all about? In a democracy, each person is responsible for evaluating the competing claims of arriving information whether it be a commercial for toothpaste, the campaign promises of a candidate, or the choice of a philosophy or religion to guide one's life. Critical thinking in a totalitarian society can lead to incarceration, torture, or death, but in a free society it is, well, critical.

Performance tests have problems of their own. They take time. They cost a lot of money. Their results can be ambiguous. There are questions about the generalizability of the performance from one context or setting to other contexts and settings.

Perhaps the most commonly used form of performance assessment is that of a portfolio. Different educators will reach different conclusions about them. What goes into one? The student's best work or typical work? Who gets to decide what's "best"? Students and teachers often differ. Should the portfolio contain different types of writing? Students tend to prefer narratives, and if they choose the contents, they are likely to be mostly stories, ignoring essays, technical reports, and poetry.

Who grades the portfolio? Different teachers might well assign different grades, something that was first noticed in 1912 (Starch & Elliott, 1912). Does this mean the portfolio is an unreliable guide? Some would say yes. Others would say no—that it reflects differences in perspective and philosophy. It might: The problem persists from publication in the classroom (putting the final draft on the bulletin board or in a booklet), to publication in journals. I have had an experience common to many writers: A submitted article to a peer-reviewed journal has been returned with every possible category checked by different reviewers—publish as is, publish with minor revision, publish with major revision, reject.

Recall the discussion in Part II, "Aspects of Achievement," about differences in willingness, and perhaps ability, to think in the United States versus in some Asian nations. Interestingly, while the Japanese secondary school is obsessed with preparation for college entrance examinations, the videotapes from the Third International Mathematics and Science Study (TIMSS) reveal middle school instruction that is more in line with performance assessment. American teachers are mostly concerned with teaching procedures and algorithms. They provide a definition and description, show students how to work the problem, provide some seatwork, and then some homework. Japanese teachers place the day's work in the context of the previous lessons. The teacher might put a problem on the blackboard and ask the students if they can apply what they have learned to solving the problem. The students work on the problem, individually at first, and then with a partner or in a small group if they choose. The teacher then invites the students who think they have solved the problem to come to the blackboard and explain their solutions.

More than one observer has wondered why the Japanese high school so industriously destroys the good pedagogy used in elementary and middle schools.

NOTES

1. The 50th percentile and other percentile ranks are often referred to as "scores." Technically, that is inaccurate, as discussed in Principle 9. Most people are aware of the distinction in this arena, and the confusion probably causes little mischief. It is cumbersome to refer constantly to "percentile ranks." "Scores" is briefer and is OK as long as we keep the real meaning of a rank in mind.

2. An exception in part is in the area of arithmetic, where the "distractors" can sometimes be built around specific errors. For instance, if the question calls for a child to find the area of a 9×4 rectangle and the child picks the answer "26," we can infer that he has confused the perimeter with the area.

CHAPTER 23

Other Indicators
of Achievement

We turn now to outcomes of education other than the commonly used tests, to examine other important aspects of schooling. E. L. Thorndike set down what remains the credo of many psychometricians: If something exists, it exists in some quantity. Against this statement, we should contrast the passage from the National Academy of Education in Part II, "Aspects of Achievement." We can also contrast it against the statement of Stanford art education professor Elliot Eisner: "some things cannot be measured, they can only be rendered" (Eisner, 1984). One wonders how Thorndike would measure, say, a Renoir, or how he would quantitatively compare a Renoir against a Picasso (or for that matter, early Picasso against late Picasso).

Not all of the indicators fit a category making them unequivocally good and the more of them the better. Some involve tradeoffs, and you will simply have to engage in higher-order thinking to decide which outcome is best for your class, school, or district.

We can characterize these other indicators in terms of whether they are student oriented, teacher oriented, parent and community oriented, or district oriented. We begin with the students.

STUDENT-BASED INDICATORS

The Percentage of Students
Taking College Admissions Tests

Our very first indicator is one that involves tradeoffs and judgment. The idea that *everyone* should go to college continues to pervade our culture. But not everyone does. Nationally, some two thirds of high school graduates do. This means about 43% don't—the graduates who don't plus the dropouts (a 1988 publication about this group was called *The Forgotten Half,* but in the decade since that publication, the proportion of graduates attending institutions of higher learning has increased significantly). What curriculum should that 43% receive?

Some, like Arthur Bestor (see Chapters 6 and 17), would argue that all should get the same curriculum no matter what their future academic endeavor might be. If it's worth teaching, said Bestor, an ardent liberal arts advocate, it's worth teaching to everyone. The goal of education for Bestor was the "disciplined mind," something that would stand people in good stead no matter where they found themselves.

More recently, Bestor has been echoed by those who argue for "high standards for everyone." This attitude is admirable at one level: It addresses our commitment to equity. But it collides with the inevitable fact of individual differences. The mantra "every student can learn" is one of the most foolish clichés to come down the pike in a long time. It is the equivalent of saying everyone can play varsity sports.

The dilemma is how to provide differential curricula without limiting life choices. In fact, it probably can't be done. Interestingly, the proliferation of school-to-work and school-to-career programs for the non-college-bound has generated opposition from some quarters. The argument is not so much that these programs limit life options, but that they are a means for providing government, business, and industry with a docile workforce, yielding to the whim of the state. To these critics, these programs are an improper encroachment of the state on individual liberty.

It is likely, however, that for the foreseeable future an increasing proportion of students taking the SAT and/or ACT will be seen by most as a positive outcome. This is true despite the recent appearance of a book lamenting not only the idea that everyone must go to college, but lamenting also the frenzy in the country to get our children into selective colleges (Lemann, 1999).

Percentage of Students Taking Advanced Placement Courses/Tests or Courses and Tests of the International Baccalaureate

AP (Advanced Placement) courses and tests are outcomes that can also be misused. These courses and their accompanying tests are developed by the College Board. A number of districts also provide "accelerated" or "advanced" courses that do not follow the specific curriculum outlined by the Board, but that adequately prepare students for AP tests.

The courses and the tests have grown tenfold in the past 20 years. Although the courses are offered in only about half of U.S. high schools, nearly 1,000,000 students take the tests (991,952 in 1998). Tests are available in 29 subjects.

The number and variety of courses/tests taken can be used as an indicator of the degree to which the district is offering a challenging curriculum.

Some districts discourage students they don't think will fare well in the course from taking it. This, I believe, is a misguided attempt to protect self-esteem. A student who takes a tough course is going to learn more than one who doesn't, including learning about what it takes to take a tough course. *Washington Post* education writer Jay Mathews (1999a) has written that

> in the last 15 years American educators have discovered that AP and IB provide a powerful way of engaging the interest not only of future Ivy Leaguers, but of otherwise indifferent students, even some juniors and sophomores who in the past would never have been considered worthy of curricular high cuisine. (p. A33)

Other educators permit perceived weaker students to take the course but discourage them from taking the test. As noted in Chapter 21, people want to look good. Some districts feel that a high pass rate on AP tests makes them look better than a high percentage of kids taking the test but with a concomitant lower pass rate.

In his book *Class Struggle,* Mathews (1999b) constructed what he called a "Challenge Index" for evaluating how properly schools are treating AP programs. The index is the size of the senior class divided by the number of AP tests taken. Mathews feels that any index exceeding 1.0 is good, and some of his most challenging schools have an index well above 2.0.

While students can "drop in" and take an AP test, they must be enrolled in an International Baccalaureate (IB) course in order to do so. The course, in turn, must be offered by an IB-authorized school that has undergone a fairly rigorous accreditation process (applying for and obtaining authorization could, itself, be taken as an indicator of achievement). The course-test tandem is required because classwork constitutes 25% of a grade in an IB class, with the test representing the other 75%.

Although the IB program is small in this country, it offers examinations in 35 different courses. The program is growing relatively quickly (but recall the distinction between rates and numbers). In 1990, American students took 4,792 IB exams, while in 1998 they sat for 13,577. Thus a near tripling of numbers still leaves the program minuscule compared to AP.

IB programs are concentrated in California, Colorado, North and South Carolina, Florida, Minnesota, New York, Texas, and Virginia. The absence of the Northeast is due to the prevalence of many private college preparatory schools that have their own tradition of curriculum development. The typical American student will take an IB test in English, a modern foreign language, a science, or perhaps a "regional history" exam—a history of Europe or a history of the Americas.

The Proportion of Students Starting "High Academic Study" in the Eighth Grade

"High academic study" is intended to differentiate such study from "the proportion of students taking algebra in eighth grade." The latter can be an indicator of a challenging curriculum, but runs against recommendations emanating from not only TIMSS but a host of domestic mathematics education reformers as well.

Traditionally, the middle school has been viewed in this country as the culmination of the primary years. It often involves a review of what was learned in elementary school. In other nations, these years constitute more the initial stages of academic study that characterizes secondary school. For instance, seventh graders in Japan receive considerable instruction in algebra while eighth grade concentrates on plane geometry. Thus, high academic study could be applied to any discipline, although it is most likely to be applied to mathematics and science.

As noted in Chapter 7, The College Board found that students who take algebra in eighth grade tended to follow a rigorous high school curriculum and to attend college. The board—and many others—made the improper causal inference that what we need to do is get more students to take algebra early. It might well be true that those who start their high academic study in the eighth grade take more rigorous study in high school and attend college. In the case of algebra, however, reformers in this country have emphasized a math curriculum that weaves algebraic concepts throughout the curriculum but that does not involve a formal course in algebra prior to high school.

For the foreseeable future, though, the proportion of students in algebra in the eighth grade is likely to serve as a proxy for a more general proportion of students in high academic study.

The Percentage of Students Going On to College or Other Postsecondary Institutions

Districts tend to report the proportion of students who go on to college. Period. This appears again to be a look-good approach, as if those attending 2-year institutions reflected poorly on the district's accomplishments.

What would be most appropriate, of course, is a highly differentiated report of postgraduate life. What proportion are in 4-year colleges, what proportion in 2-year, what proportion in the military, what proportion obtain employment in other than low-skill, dead-end jobs? What proportion *are* doing hamburger-flipper type work and what proportion are living at home, unemployed?

These statistics should be presented in the context of the local economy. This might be the most wonderful national economy ever (so sayeth Federal Reserve Board Chairman Alan Greenspan), but not all sectors and not all geographic areas experience the same degree of wonderfulness.

How Do Students Fare at Institutions of Higher Education?

It's one thing to send students to college. It's something else to keep them there. Is the district's college drop-out rate lower than the average for a particular college? It is important to differentiate among colleges, because those who attend private schools and the flagship universities in a state system typically have much lower drop-out rates than those who attend other institutions.

Beyond knowing the college drop-out rate and, conversely, the graduation rate—or even the postgraduate attendance rate—it should be possible to obtain information on how well the students are performing. I say "should be" because I don't know of any place where this is being done other than informally—college admissions staff reporting back to high school counselors in personal communications.

When I worked in a school district in Colorado, the state universities were, by law, supposed to provide such information. Most did not and the only one I recall that did, provided relatively primitive information: The grade point average (GPA) of our students compared to the GPA of all enrollees.

But that time was eons ago in terms of the costs and sophistication of information technology. It should be possible now to develop inexpensive yet more comprehensive protocols for telling high schools how their students are faring.

In a recent publication, Clifford Adelman (1999) of the U.S. Department of Education has concentrated on a seldom used indicator: college completion. Adelman constructs an index called ACRES (standing for ACademic RESources). ACRES expresses what Adelman calls the intensity and the quality of the high school curriculum. *Intensity* refers to how many academic course credits are acquired, while *quality* refers to the final level attained, especially in mathematics and laboratory sciences. ACRES is the single best predictor of college completion, outperforming both test scores and high school GPA/rank.

Percentage of Students
Meeting State Mandates

These mandates come in a variety of forms. In the early days after *A Nation at Risk,* a number of states created "honors diplomas" or "governor's diplomas," a sheepskin that required something more than the "core" requirements needed to graduate. Typically, these diplomas require 4 years of math, English, and social studies, 3 of science, and at least 2 of a foreign language.

More recently, the mandates have come solely in the form of tests. As noted in the section on uses of tests, the mandates carry a variety of sanctions, mostly punitive for failure, less often recognition for conspicuous success. In some states, the mandate specifies a certain score on a test or a certain percentage of the students attaining a specified score. Less often, the initial administration of a state testing program is taken as a baseline from which progress is to be measured (recall, trends vs. snapshots).

The extent to which meeting the mandate is a desirable indicator of achievement depends on the degree to which people agree that the mandate causes the right things to be taught in the schools. For instance, most people in Virginia seem satisfied that, social studies aside, the standards in the Standards of Learning program are good ones. There is much less agreement about the tests. Although the tests have adequate psychometric properties in terms of reliability and validity, many people view them as regressive because of their fact-oriented, multiple-choice format. Some also object to the specific facts that the students are required to learn, feeling them to be relatively trivial.

These attitudes appear elsewhere in slogans such as "Bleep the MEAP" (Michigan Educational Assessment Program), "Toss the TAAS" (Texas Assessment of Academic Skills), and "Erase the CASE" (Chicago Academic Standards Examination). There are reports from various states of parents, teachers, and students organizing to resist the tests. As this is written, the standards movement has clearly run amok (Bracey, 1999a).

Drop-Out and School Completion Rates

It is doubtful that there is a squishier statistic in education than the drop-out rate. That is too bad, because the drop-out rate is increasingly important to know. Gary Orfield at Harvard University

sity has noted that, nationally, the drop-out rate has been rising for whites, blacks, and Hispanics. He wonders if the increase is associated with the standards movement (Orfield, 2000). Certainly increased incidence of retaining students in grade would lead to increased drop-out rates. In 1994, Milwaukee established an algebra-for-all policy. More than half of the students fail, and it is likely that this accounts for the large increase in the number of ninth graders who have too few credits to be declared tenth graders. It is not clear how, or if, this is affecting drop-out rates, but clearly there has been a large increase in the number of Milwaukee ninth graders experiencing failure at the beginning of their high school careers.

Moreover, the algebra-for-all program does not seem to have affected achievement at the upper end of the spectrum: While more students are taking AP courses, not many more are taking the tests, and those who do mostly do not obtain high scores.

There are a variety of ways of calculating drop-out and graduation rates. The U.S. Department of Education defines a dropout as a person aged 16 to 24 who does not have a high school diploma or the equivalent and who is not enrolled in school. This is probably not a workable definition for localities.

Some districts define a dropout as someone who leaves the school and for whom the school has obtained no request for transcripts after some prescribed period of time. This definition depends on accurate record keeping and diligent record processing. In urban areas with high poverty and high mobility, resources are usually inadequate to keep up.

It is possible to define drop-out rate and school completion rate as the size of the ninth grade class divided into the size of the senior class. This works well only for highly stable districts or for districts where the net in-migration is zero, that is, where an equal number of new students arrive to replace those who leave (20% of all students change school each year).

Some districts also calculate the on-time graduation rate along with a graduation rate at some later point in time. This allows for those who drop out and return or who obtain an equivalent such as the GED to be entered into the graduation rate.

Promotion and Retention Rates

While perhaps not a measure of "achievement," promotion and retention rates deserve attention because they do impact on other indicators. As noted, retaining a student in a grade increases probability of the student later dropping out. Thus, if a district has a policy of lowering drop-out rates, a policy of ending "social promotion" would likely be in direct conflict.

As noted earlier, a policy of increasing test scores can be impacted by the retention-promotion policy. If the test occurs at eighth grade, retaining low-performing students at the end of the seventh grade will increase the test scores. The "increase" is spurious, of course, coming from the retention of children who score low.

A common argument in favor of ending social promotion is that if children know they don't have to work to get by, they won't. In some instances this is probably true, but it ignores the complex relationship of the child and the school. Those who argue that this occurs have as yet not produced any research evidence to support it.

Attendance Rates, Students and Staff

The attendance rate of staff is one index of morale. The attendance rates for students are more complex but should also be examined in terms of morale. Many absences at the elementary level are disturbing because they almost always involve the complicity of parents.

Policy decisions about attendance, test scores, and dropouts can work against each other and indicate the need for a "composite index" discussed in Chapter 14. In Chicago, high schools used to keep students with many absences on the rolls. Some say this is because the schools were encouraging the students to stay in school. Others say this is because schools wanted the enrollment to keep teacher positions. With a new administration emphasizing both test scores and attendance, however, many of these students are now being dropped from the rolls. Getting rid of them simultaneously improves attendance rates and test scores. Said an assistant principal at one school, "What we have found is those kids who are missing 20 days are the ones that drag your test scores down. The school is penalized statistically for those kids. We want quality more than quantity. If that means removing dead weight, we will remove dead weight" (Kelleher, 1999, p. 1).

Thus, the "drop-out rate" in Chicago is soaring, the attendance rate is improving, and test scores are rising. All of these outcomes, however, reflect only a shifting emphasis on what counts in accountability.

TEACHER-BASED INDICATORS

Percentage of Teachers With Majors or Minors in Areas of Teaching Responsibility

"You can't teach what you don't know," goes the old saying. Beyond this simple statement lurks complexity. We probably all know college professors who can't teach what they do know. In addition, there are questions about how much a teacher, especially an elementary teacher, needs to be steeped in a specific discipline. How much mathematics does a third-grade teacher need? After all, she also has to teach all of the other curriculum topics except art and music, and maybe those as well. What is likely—and this is opinion—is that a teacher at any level needs to have some appreciation of what it means to be steeped in a specific discipline.

Currently some 23% of all secondary school teachers do not have even a minor in their main area of teaching responsibility. This average, like many, masks important differences. While the figure is only 8% for teachers in low-poverty schools, it is more than one third in high-poverty schools. Any use of this statistic as an indicator of achievement must take the demographics of the school into account.

Again, this is an indicator that can be in conflict with other indicators, in this case, with class size. California initiated a $1.5 billion annual expense to get the state's class size down to 20 from an average of 30. This set off a wave of panicky hiring since schools receive money for each child who is in a small class ($850 at the moment). With teaching slots opening up in the suburbs, teachers fled inner cities, leaving the poorer districts (a) hiring people with "emergency certification" and (b) unable to implement the class size reduction as fast as the suburbs could. The latter had the impact of further preventing money from flowing into the poor schools because the money was contingent on small classes (Stecher & Bohrnstedt, 1999).

Percentage of Teachers With Regular Certification

This indicator is influenced by different mandates in different states. As noted, the legislation mandating small class sizes in

California produced a great increase in applications for emergency teaching certification in that state. In other states, a prevailing view that "anyone can teach" has produced legislation or regulation permitting various kinds of "alternative certification."

There is also, at the current time, much controversy about the certification process in schools of education. Another cliche with some truth to it to emerge from TIMSS is that "the United States has one of the best educated and poorest trained teaching forces in the world." By this is meant that more than half of our teachers have attained master's degrees, far more than in other countries, but that the United States lacks long-term mentoring and/or internship programs for future teachers.

Some trenchant comments on the teacher preparation process occur in the report of the National Commission on Teaching and America's Future, *What Matters Most:*

> Although no state will permit a person to fix plumbing, guard swimming pools, style hair, design a building, or practice medicine without completing training and passing an examination, more than 40 states allow districts to hire teachers on emergency licenses who have not met these basic requirements. States pay more attention to the qualifications of veterinarians treating the nation's cats and dogs than to those of teachers educating the nation's children and youth. (National Commission on Teaching and America's Future, 1996, p. 14)

People have been complaining about teacher preparation for at least a quarter century, maybe longer, but little seems to change. The latest lament is from the Education Trust, which analyzed the content of teacher licensing exams and found them wanting: Virtually none of the questions covered college-level material. It must be pointed out, however, that people who *review* tests invariably think that the tests are easier than those who have to *confront* the test by actually taking it.

People sometimes take curious positions on teacher licensing and certification. For example, Diane Ravitch (1999), in an *Education Week* op-ed essay, unfavorably compared the progress of medicine from medical research to the lack of progress of education based on educational research. Yet Ravitch was one of the signatories to a Fordham Foundation "manifesto" prescribing how to obtain "the teachers we need." Medicine is a highly regulated field, yet one of the premises of the manifesto was that teaching should be de-regulated to open the field to content experts with no teaching credentials (Fordham Foundation, 1999).

Teacher Experience and Expertise

The last item in the previous exposition noted that teacher licensing tests don't demand much of teachers. The research on teacher education levels is mixed—some find it matters, some don't. It likely depends on what was studied in the advanced education: material to make the person a better teacher or simply a more highly paid one. A number of classes that count toward a master's degree in some institutions have little connection with improving the teachers' classroom performance.

The research on teacher experience is more consistent: More experienced teachers get better results. In the lore of schools, there is a curvilinear relationship between experience and outcomes. Inexperienced teachers have not mastered their craft well enough, those approaching retirement have lost their fire and are even burned out. I know of no research that has tried to gather actual evidence on this widespread belief.

Recently, new information on "value-added" teaching has caught many an eye. This research is discussed in detail in Chapter 32. We note here that University of Tennessee researcher Williams Sanders grouped teachers into quintiles according to their ability to produce test score gains in children from fall to spring. Students with very test-effective teachers gained considerably more than students with ineffective teachers. The impact could still be seen two grades later (Sanders & Rivers, 1996). This research and its implications are discussed in Part III, Chapter 32, in the question about accountability.

We note here that none of the research has yet moved to the crucial task of identifying what it is about these teachers that makes them "effective" or not. Are they focused on material covered by the test? Do they really know their stuff? Do they have some extra ability to get it across to students?

NOTA BENE: The value-added system as developed in Tennessee would require the testing of every child in every subject every year. This would have multiple consequences. In the first place, it would likely increase the district's testing costs a great deal. Second, it would require the use of multiple-choice tests to keep from busting that budget. Third, it could easily distort the accountability system by overemphasizing the role of testing.

Professional Development Activities for Teachers

Professional development activities can come from internal action as well as external.

A number of studies have noted that Japanese teachers have a longer school day but a shorter teaching day than American teachers. They have time to think about what they're doing. American teachers mostly do not (in part because American textbooks are about three times as thick as those in other nations). In addition, teachers in Japan and other nations have more collegial approaches to teaching than American teachers, for whom it is often a quite solitary profession. In Japan, one room in a school is reserved for planning and collegial conversation. It is not a "teachers' lounge."

External activities are often too short for effective learning that results in long-term consequences. One teacher described Professional Development Days as days when "Some guy blows in, blows off, and blows out." A day-long inservice needn't be ineffectual, but such days must be followed up with relevant activities that sustain whatever was learned on the day itself.

Professional development activities, especially external ones, have come under scrutiny of late because of the feeling that teachers should be in class, teaching. Yet real professional development activities are satisfying, and the absence of them would no doubt lead to stagnation. At a conference on privatization, syndicated columnist Mona Charen lamented that teachers in her district had Wednesday afternoons "off" for training. "One would have thought they were trained when they were hired," Charen whined. Off course, it is likely that Charen's physician and dentist attend professional development courses. It is curious that such development is not only tolerated but encouraged in these fields, but not as well in teaching.

One solution to actually closing up shop for a half day is to provide students with activities that people agree are meaningful but that are conducted by someone other than teachers. For example, at the Key School in Indianapolis, teachers gather after lunch on Wednesdays and spend the rest of the afternoon in a planning and evaluation meeting. They might be planning what they're going to do tomorrow, next week, or next year.

In the meantime, parent volunteers accompany the children to the auditorium to see presentations about what various occupations do. Once when I was visiting, nurses and paramedics were explaining the nature of their jobs and the kinds of skills required. During another visit, a quartet from the Indianapolis Symphony played, described their instruments, and talked about how they learned to play them (all students at the Key School learn to play a musical instrument).

PARENT- AND COMMUNITY-BASED INDICATORS

Contact With the Community

The discussion of the community visitors leads naturally into broader discussion of community contacts. These can either bring the community into the school or take the school out to the community. Either way, community contacts are an important indicator of achievement. They indicate the extent to which the school breaks down the natural isolation of the school and the extent to which it realizes that learning occurs in many settings, not just classrooms.

The opportunity for such contacts, of course, will vary considerably from community to community. Not everyone lives in close proximity to a symphony that can send some members over to the school. Indeed, it would seem worthwhile to construct a list of available community resources—museums, libraries, universities, businesses, industries—and a list of those resources that the school is making use of. The resulting resource-utilization ratio ought to decrease over time—unless, of course, new resources are becoming available.

The Internet would seem to offer almost unlimited resources for expanding the definition of "community." For instance, students all over the world constructed mirrors that were assembled into a basketball sized satellite that was then launched by NASA from the space shuttle. The astronauts deliberately put the satellite into an imperfect orbit so it would lose altitude each day. Students use the changes to measure the density of the upper atmosphere (this project is described in more detail below under "Average Age of Textbooks."

Level of "Consumer" Satisfaction
With a District's Graduates

"Consumer" is in quotes because school is not a service like any other—although those advocating market-driven schooling argue that it ought to be and simplistically reduce it to such. Who in the school setting is the consumer? The military, business and industry, and institutions of higher education that receive the "product" after graduation? The parents? The students themselves? The next grade teacher in relation to what she is receiving from the earlier grade?

Although there is some utility in looking at all of these as consumers, there is really a basic flaw in the metaphor. Ultimately, it takes one back to the false conception of the school as a factory, of kids as raw material, and graduates as "product." Although no one would think of their own children as "raw material" and "product" (I hope), when people think of "students" in the abstract, they drift into the factory model quite easily. As Denise Gelberg (1997) showed in *The "Business" of Reforming American Schools,* businessmen have encouraged such thinking for more than a century.

Still, there can be some utility in examining the satisfaction of the various "clients" receiving graduates. It just must be done with some reality checks in mind. Professors and businessmen are as prone to the nostalgic, know-nothing-kids mentality as anyone. The military appears to have largely got past it. If, for instance, you hear of university disappointment in your students, you could match it against (a) SAT and ACT scores and, (b) if how students fare at institutions of higher education is considered, grades. How do your students stack up against others applying for admission? How does their GPA compare with the school as a whole?

Similarly, a complaint from business needs to be matched against the reality of the jobs offered. On the op-ed page of the *Washington Post* a few years ago, Alan Wurtzel, the chairman of the board at Circuit City, a large discount electronics corporation, wrote that "in hiring new employees for our stores, warehouses, and offices, Circuit City is looking for people who are able to provide very high levels of customer service, who are honest, and who have a positive, enthusiastic, achievement-oriented work ethic." Wurtzel claimed Circuit City seldom found these qualities in American high school graduates. When I called the Personnel Office at

Circuit City, I found that new hires received minimum wage except for the sales force, which worked strictly on commission (Wurtzel, 1993).

It does not seem unreasonable to suggest that for that kind of money, Mr. Wurtzel and his ilk should be in the business of *producing* those qualities through on-the-job training rather than expecting to find them in people who are willing to work for minimum wage.

Similarly, Sam Ginn, CEO of Pacific Telesis, liked to tell audiences he gave a reading test to 8,400 applicants and only 2,800 scored high enough that he would be willing to hire them. He did not tell audiences that his jobs paid $7 an hour or $14,000 a year. This calculation is based on a 40-hour week and 50-week year. Actually, since the employers are no longer required to pay benefits to employees who work less than 34 hours a week, the amount of part-time employment has soared. It is not clear that the jobs in question were full-time.

Parents can be surveyed, and many districts and schools make use of this technique to obtain feedback about how the community feels about the school's operation. Students can be surveyed as well at various points in time after graduation. We should note that it is important to ensure that there is an adequate rate of return of the surveys. People who don't return surveys differ in their attitudes from those who do. How can we know this, you might ask—if they don't send the surveys back, we don't know how they feel. Some researches have dug into this issue by following up with a phone call or door-to-door survey.

The level of parent involvement in school activities and functions is one of the best indicators of how well a school has achieved a good relationship with the community. This indicator is highly conditioned by demographics, though. In one diverse district, the wealthy sector conducted PTA meetings during the school day—mothers were either at home or had occupations that permitted them to leave the workplace. Fathers had similar occupations. In the poorer section of the district, though, schools used various sorts of enticements—bingo, pizza, and so on—to encourage attendance, but with little success. Many parents in this part of the district were single parents and many worked two jobs as well. Attitude surveys indicated that they maintained intense interest in their children's education and expected them to attend college, but their days left them too drained to attend the meetings. Nationally, membership in PTAs and PTOs is plummeting, and the culprit most often fingered is the two-working-parent family.

RESOURCE INDICATORS

Average Age of Textbooks

Back in 1994, I heard a story on NPR's *All Things Considered* that some Alabama textbooks predicted that man might one day walk on the moon. In 1999, another story on *All Things Considered* stated that those predictions were also found in some California textbooks still on library shelves. The fiscal cutbacks emanating from Proposition 13 (which limited increases in real estate taxes) have had many adverse effects in California, but none more perverse than on the holdings of the schools libraries.

Age is less important in some areas than others. Readings in English courses change slowly; the topics investigated by science often do not. In June 1999 a satellite was deployed from NASA's space shuttle that permitted children all over the world to calculate the upper atmosphere's density. About the size of a medicine ball, the satellite was constructed of 878 aluminum mirrors polished by students to make the orb visible to the naked eye by reflecting sunshine. Its orbit is such that aerodynamic drag causes it to get a little shorter each day. Students are using the changes to infer the atmosphere's density:

> Student observers are measuring the satellite's right ascension and declination at precise times by reference to known stars, and they are recording the precise timing of their observation by the use of stopwatches synchronized with international time signals such as Radio Station WWWV in the USA. They are using GPS receivers or United States Geological Survey 7½ minute quadrangle maps, or their equivalent in other countries to post the latitude, longitude and altitude of their observing sites. They are posting their observations on the project's web site to permit computation of the classical elements of the satellite's orbit by the angles-only method of LaPlace. (*www. azinet.com/ starshine/descript.htm*)

Gee. We didn't do that sorta stuff in my school. It's a good paragraph to read the next time someone starts yearning for the good ol' days. You might also take down "A Beginner's Guide on How to Track Starshine" and see how many people can follow the directions. They don't seem to be poorly written (*http://spacekids.hq. nasa.gov/starshine/guide_beg.htm*).

They do seem to call for complex skills that were not taught in schools in the "good ol' days."

An equity suit in Alabama also revealed that some districts had no textbooks, and some had insufficient numbers to permit the assignment of homework. The culprit here is poverty, of course, and these conditions hold in many places other than Alabama. Along with age, though, a textbook-to-pupil ratio determination might be in order.

Interestingly, the first experiment of Project Starshine was conducted by Scott Stepko, a middle schooler in Madison, Alabama. Madison is a suburb of Huntsville. Huntsville is where they build rockets, so I guess they also get first dibs on the latest textbooks and equipment (and parents who really are rocket scientists).

Adequacy of Scientific Laboratory and Field Equipment

Adequacy is related to but not identical to age. Some of the equipment used for Project Starshine is state of the art, such as computers, the Internet, and global positioning satellites. Some of it is more traditional: flashlights, tape, and compasses.

It seems likely that the essentials of the scientific process can be taught with almost anything, since the task is to present science as a detective story, and the emphasis is on how the detective works as much as on what he or she finds. Teaching astronomy, on the other hand, will likely be helped by computer programs such as "Dance of the Planets" that present graphic representations not possible in a book.

Science appears to be an area where students are particularly prone to developing misconceptions about how the world works. Some of these misconceptions come from the static models in books, some come from everyday experience—much of contemporary science is counter-intuitive to such experience. And some of it comes from misunderstanding what has been presented. For example, in the Annenberg/PBS videotape series, *Minds of Our Own,* one fifth grader described as very inquisitive explains how we see. The model he has developed he obtained from a science television program on vision. The program showed how light bounces off objects and into our eyes and this is what enables us to see the objects. The student, though, got the impression that we *emit* the light from our eyes, which then bounces off objects and back into our eyes. He likens it to a bat's "radar" system of hearing.

The series offers fascinating glimpses into how children's minds work—even honors students in advanced physics classes don't "get" what we try to teach them. The misunderstandings are often invisible to even successful veteran teachers because of teaching by lecturing and testing with multiple-choice questions. The series also offers information on how to teach science to ensure that the misconceptions are dealt with. The series can be located at *www. learner.org* or at 1-800-965-7373.

Effective Use of Technology

Project Starshine looks like an effective use of technology. A scandalous story a few years ago in the *Washington Post* described a large inventory of computers, all hidden away in a closet and never unpacked. This is not an effective use of technology. Beyond that, a study from ETS (Educational Testing Service) found that students who used computers in drill and practice exercises actually did worse than those who learned arithmetic with traditional techniques. Students who used computers for more sophisticated problem solving did better than their traditional peers.

This study must be considered only suggestive, however, because it is in all likelihood confounded with social class. Students assigned computers for drill and practice these days are likely low performers in poor schools. Still, there should be descriptions of what the technology is being used for.

The effective use of technology by *teachers* should also be examined. Some teachers still do not know much about technology and are afraid to start using it lest they show how much more the students know than they do. Others are technology enthusiasts. Without care, these enthusiasts can become isolated from the techno-phobes. With proper planning, they can be used as catalysts to introduce technology on a wider scale.

Class Size

The day this section was first written, an Associated Press wire story appeared in some papers declaring that smaller class size was no panacea. Actually, the study replicated the findings of Project STAR, indicating that smaller classes were more effective up to fourth grade. Project STAR, reducing some classes to a range of 13 to 17 in grades K-3, also found that the impact was not only sustained but cumulative—students in small classes were farther ahead of their regular class peers in seventh grade than in sixth, and so on.

The effects of class size reductions were discussed briefly under Principle 2, "Follow the Money" (Chapter 2). Here we must emphasize that "reduction in class size" is not the same thing as "declining pupil-teacher ratio." Declining pupil-teacher ratio has been a naturally occurring phenomenon for some years now. The national figure is around 17:1. Average class size, however, is about 23 students for each teacher in the primary years and 25 in the secondary years. The difference is that P-T ratio is calculated using all people with teaching certificates. This includes not only teachers with particularly small classes, such as special education and Limited English Proficiency teachers, but also certificated staff who have no classroom responsibilities. It is not clear whether there is a "threshold effect" for class size reduction, but most people think that a class size of 23, the national average, is still too large to offer much in the way of improved achievement.

Class size reduction (CSR), on the other hand, at least from studies like Project STAR and Project SAGE, is an *experimental* outcome (Finn & Achilles, 1999). In STAR, the schools were not chosen randomly because the state could not compel schools to participate, but within each participating school, students and teachers in grades K-3 were assigned randomly to regular class rooms, regular classrooms with a full-time teacher's aide, or to small classes (13-17 students).

Students in the smaller classrooms achieved more than those in regular classrooms. Students in classes with teacher's aides gained more, too, but not nearly as much as those in small classes. The effects have not only been sustained into high school, but cumulative: Students who were in small classes were farther ahead of their peers at grade 8 than at grade 6. Here are some of the results:

	Grade 4	*Grade 6*	*Grade 8*
Mathematics	5.9 mos.	8.4 mos.	1 yr., 1 mo.
Reading	9.1 mos.	9.2 mos.	1 yr., 2 mos.
Science	7.6 mos.	6.7 mos.	1 yr., 1 mo.

Eric Hanushek has claimed that the effect occurs only at kindergarten and that it is a "fixed" effect over time. He contends (with no evidence whatsoever) that it probably occurs because children in small kindergarten classes find it easier to learn the rituals and routines of a place called school. The reason Hanushek's and others' analyses differ has to do with the metrics used. Hanushek's metric of choice is effect size, a perfectly legitimate statistic. However, it is a statistic with different characteristics than some of the other statistics used to measure educational growth. A fixed effect size over time for small classes, for example would mean that the small-class students were moving farther and farther ahead of their peers in terms of, say, grade equivalents.

Project SAGE, a CSR experiment in Milwaukee, also finds achievement gains from small classes (Molnar et al., 1999). In addition, SAGE begins to ask the important question: Why? Why do small classes achieve more? Teachers in SAGE reported that they could get to know the children better and attend to each child more frequently. Discipline problems did not disappear, but the small classes had more of a "family" atmosphere and such problems were reduced. Teachers reported more "individualization," but in further discussion, it became clear that this meant paying attention to individuals in order that they might master the material, not permitting students to follow their own lines of interest.

The above are teacher reports. They need to be corroborated with observations of actual behavior. Still, studies using only natural, not experimental, class size reduction found that teachers deploy their time differently and use different strategies in smaller classes, even though the classes involved were mostly high school courses (experimental CSRs have been exclusively in elementary schools).

One thing that is not often noticed about Project STAR is that it did not conduct any professional development activities to inform teachers about how to take advantage of smaller classes. If such training were available, the effects of small classes might be even larger.

The post-STAR debate over class size reductions has been cast entirely in terms of cognitive outcomes. This overlooks the results of the original class size meta-analysis suggesting that *affective* outcomes start appearing earlier. That is, a class size reduction from, say, 25 to 21 will produce a larger increase in affective outcomes than cognitive outcomes. People like to teach in and be in small classes.

The impact of small classes might turn out to be "robust." The small-class mandate in California has a lot going against it, but the initial findings showed small gains over all. Among the things going against the mandate were a shortage of classroom teachers. This existing shortage was a disaster for poor districts—as teaching positions opened up in suburbs, some of the better teachers left cities for those positions. There was an enormous increase in requests for "emergency certification" in poor districts.

Hanushek (1999) has recently also commented that "Japanese class sizes are much larger than U.S. class sizes. Japanese student performance is, on average, much better than U.S. student performance" (p. 147). However, a Japanese educator, reviewing tapes of American and Japanese teachers teaching, concluded that the Japanese teachers were not more effective than American teachers—although they were more problem oriented in contrast to the American focus on procedures and algorithms. The Japanese teachers, he commented, could count on their students spending considerable time out of school on math problems. Most of them would studiously attend to their homework. Most of them would also attend a *juku*—a cram school that concentrates on teaching students to take tests. Japanese kids, he said, score higher than American children largely because of what happens outside of school.

PART III

Handling the
Tough Questions

This part of the book focuses on data that bear on some commonly asked questions that reflect some commonly held misconceptions about the performance of American schools. We should repeat, though, that the earlier two sections, especially Part I, also contained relevant data.

The Principle "Follow the Money" also addressed the questions "Why are we throwing money at the schools?" and "Why don't we use vouchers?"

The Principle "Watch for Selectivity in the Data" could be said to address the question "Why is the number of high scorers on the SAT falling?"

The Principle "Beware of Nostalgia" could be rephrased as "Why don't kids know as much as they used to?"

"Make sure the statistic used is the right one" in part answers the question, "Why do we spend more money on our schools than other nations?"

"Beware of 'clean' data" offers an answer to the question, "Why do Americans believe in ability while Asians believe in effort?"

The opening section of "Aspects of Achievement" answers, "Why don't we restructure our schools along the lines of high-scoring Asian systems?"

The sections on drop-out and retention rates offer evidence bearing on a question, "Why don't we end 'social promotion'?"

CHAPTER 24

How Come American Students Fall Farther Behind Their International Peers the Longer They Stay in School?

Short Answer: There apparently is some slippage between grades 4 and 8 in mathematics and science, but not in reading. There might well not be any further fall back. If there is, it likely has to do with the larger culture rather than with what schools offer.

In order to understand this question fully, we need to know where it came from. It arose after the TIMSS (Third International Mathematics and Science Study) fourth-grade data were reported in 1997 and compared to the eighth-grade data released in 1996 (Mullis et al., 1997; Martin et al., 1997; Beaton, Martin, Mullis et al., 1996; Beaton, Mullis, Martin et al., 1996). In the fourth grade, American students were 12th of 26 nations in math, and third of 26 in science. At the eighth grade, they were average among the 41 nations in both subjects, being slightly above average in science and slightly below average in math. President Clinton, among others, seized on these results to claim that we were the only nation that fell from above average to below between fourth and eighth grade.

The TIMSS final year report appeared in early 1998 (Mullis et al., 1998). The way it was released, it appeared to be an apples-to-apples comparison in which our 12th graders were very low, and even our best 12th graders were near the bottom. *Appeared* is the operative word. The final year study was so flawed in so many ways that the data are virtually uninterpretable. Where I have managed to tease out the subgroups of American students who were most like their international peers, I find no further decline from grade 8: Americans finished in the middle of the pack.

Actually, we might have been average in math at all three levels. Seven of the nations that outscored the United States in mathematics at the eighth-grade level did not participate at the fourth-grade level. If we assume that they would have scored higher at the fourth-grade level, then the U.S. performance there becomes quite average, as it was at the eighth-grade level.

The pattern looks different for science: Most countries that participated at both grades had similar scores at both levels. Singapore was an exception, rising 60 points; and the United States was unusual as well, falling 30 points.

These scores, as noted in Principle 1, are averages, and there is enormous variability around them. In addition, the overall tests were composed of subtests. The performance of American students and those in other countries varies a great deal depending on the subtest. That is, while the overall score was average, American students did very well on some subtests, very poorly on others. This was true of students in other nations as well.

This strongly implies a commonsense conclusion: Children learn what they are taught, and they are taught different things in different countries. How else to explain the performance of children in France, who did very well in TIMSS math, very well in a reading study discussed below, but 27th of 41 nations in TIMSS science? Surely one would not wish to argue that French brains can accommodate math and reading but not scientific concepts. Indeed, while the curriculum studies from TIMSS in math and science were both titled *Many Visions, Many Aims,* the visions and aims seem more variable across countries in science than in math.

If we look to reading, the fall in American performance happens or doesn't happen, depending on whether you look at ranks or scores (see Principle 9). In 1992, the same organization that conducted TIMSS released a reading study, *How in the World Do Students*

Read. American 9-year-olds were second among 27 nations, American 14-year-olds were eighth (Elley, 1996).

Those are the ranks. The scores tell a different tale. American 9-year-olds scored 547, while top-ranked Finland came in at 569. At the upper age, Finnish students scored 560, while American students scored 535. The scale used was identical to that of the SAT—a mean of 500, a standard deviation of 100.

Looking at *scores,* the American students were 22 points out of first place as 9-year-olds, 25 points out of first place as 14-year-olds. On a 600-point scale, this 3-point change hardly looks like a decline. In fact, only the score of first-place Finland was statistically significantly higher. The countries were so tightly bunched that the scores of the nations from 2nd through 16th place did not differ significantly from the U.S. score. Most of the nations that scored ahead of the United States had trailed closely behind at the younger age, the major exception being Hungary, which improved its score from 499 to 536 and its ranking from 20th to 5th.

The curriculum analyses in TIMSS strongly suggest that the American middle school curricula in mathematics and science, especially math, need revamping (see "Proportion of Students in High Academic Study" in Chapter 23). For too many American students, middle school represents the culmination of elementary grades, with a lot of boring review. In other nations, the middle years are the beginning of intense academic study and concentrate on algebra and geometry (Schmidt, McKnight, Valverde et al., 1996; Schmidt, Raizen, Britton et al., 1996). We actually did not need TIMSS to tell us this. Math educators have been saying it for as long as I can remember.

In addition, the curriculum analyses showed that American math and science textbooks are about three times as thick as those in other nations. In America, textbooks are developed by commercial publishers. Wanting to sell to as many markets as possible, these publishers write kitchen-sink textbooks rather than texts that present a single, coherent approach to a topic.

American teachers are cowed by the tyranny of scope and sequence and attempt to teach it all. The result is that coverage is often brief and shallow. The vaunted "spiral curriculum" turns out to be mostly a circle: Teachers keep coming back to the same topics in advancing grades because not enough time has been spent for the topic to "sink in" (there is something to be said for the role of memorization).

TABLE 24.1   TIMSS Middle School Science Results (1996)

1.	**Singapore**	**70**
2.	Korea	66
3.	Japan	65
4.	Czech Republic	64
6.	Bulgaria	62
6.	Netherlands	62
6.	Slovenia	62
9.	England	61
9.	Hungary	61
9.	Austria	61
11.5.	Belgium (Fl.)	60
11.5.	Australia	60
14.	Slovak Republic	59
14.	Sweden	59
14.	Canada	59
19.	Ireland	58
19.	**United States**	**58**
19.	Russian Federation	58
19.	New Zealand	58
19.	Norway	58
19.	Hong Kong	58
19.	Germany	58
23.5.	Thailand	57
23.5.	Israel	57
25.5.	Switzerland	56
International Average = 56		
25.5.	Spain	56
27.	Scotland	55
28.	France	54
29.5.	Greece	52
29.5.	Iceland	52
31.	Denmark	51
33.5.	Latvia	50
33.5.	Portugal	50
33.5.	Belgium (Fr.)	50
33.5.	Romania	50
36.	Lithuania	49
37.5.	Iran	47
37.5.	Cyprus	47
39.	Kuwait	43
40.	Columbia	39
41.	**South Africa**	**27**

Teachers in other nations spend more time on a topic, but then do not revisit it as American teachers do. It would seem that a combination of the two approaches would produce the most desir-

TABLE 24.2   TIMSS Middle School Math Results (1996)

1.	**Singapore**	79
2.	Japan	73
3.	Korea	72
4.	Hong Kong	70
5.5.	Belgium (Fl.)	66
5.5.	Czech Republic	66
8.5.	Slovak Republic	62
8.5.	Switzerland	62
8.5.	Hungary	62
8.5.	Austria	62
11.5.	France	61
11.5.	Slovenia	61
14.	Russian Federation	60
14.	Bulgaria	60
14.	Netherlands	60
17.	Canada	59
17.	Ireland	59
17.	Belgium (Fr.)	59
20.	Australia	58
21.5.	Thailand	57
21.5.	Israel	57
23.	Sweden	56
International Average = 55		
25.	Norway	54
25.	Germany	54
27.5.	**United States**	53
27.5.	England	53
29.5.	Scotland	52
29.5.	Denmark	52
31.5.	Latvia	51
31.5.	Spain	51
33.	Iceland	50
34.5.	Greece	49
34.5.	Romania	49
36.5.	Lithuania	48
36.5.	Cyprus	48
37.	Portugal	43
39.	Iran	38
40.	Columbia	29
10.	South Africa	24

able results. Teachers should spend more time on a topic *and* revisit it.

As noted, the TIMSS final year report entered the popular culture as an apples-to-apples comparison. Our 12th graders went up against their 12th graders and got trounced. Our best 12th graders

TABLE 24.3   TIMSS Fourth Grade Science Results

Korea	74
Japan	70
Netherlands	67
United States	66
Australia	66
Austria	66
Czech Republic	65
Singapore	65
Canada	64
Slovenia	64
England	63
Hong Kong	62
Hungary	62
Ireland	61
Norway	60
New Zealand	60
Scotland	60
Israel	57
Latvia	56
Iceland	55
Greece	54
Cyprus	51
Portugal	50
Thailand	49
Kuwait	39
Iran	40

went up against their best 12th graders and got trounced. That is not what happened. It wasn't even an apples-to-oranges comparison. As noted in the know-nothing-kids principle, it was more like apples to aardvarks.

In most countries today, you can count on virtually everyone being in school through the eighth grade and receiving the same curriculum. That ceases to be true as students enter what is referred to in most countries as upper secondary school. In some countries, a substantial proportion of the students leave before the end of secondary school. While the U.S. Department of Education argued that the enrollments in most countries were "roughly comparable," some nations had an aggregate enrollment for ages 12 to 17 as low as 77% of all eligibles. "Roughly comparable" is not adequately precise for a research study in any case, but one can only wonder how many of the tested students, mostly over age 18, were still in school.

TABLE 24.4   TIMSS Fourth Grade Mathematics Results

Korea	76
Singapore	76
Japan	74
Hong Kong	73
Netherlands	69
Czech Republic	66
Austria	65
Slovenia	64
Hungary	64
Ireland	63
United States	63
Australia	63
Canada	60
Israel	59
Latvia	59
Scotland	58
England	57
Cyprus	54
Norway	53
New Zealand	53
Greece	51
Iceland	50
Thailand	50
Portugal	48
Iran	38
Kuwait	32

Most nations do not have comprehensive high schools with greater or lesser tracking. Their upper secondary programs are clearly differentiated. In some nations, as many as half of all eighth graders enter a vocational track. In Germany, for instance, only 31% of the students are enrolled in a program that could lead to a college education.

Ignoring for a moment that only 6 of the 21 nations participating in the final year study met the TIMSS criteria for valid data, we see that American students scored 461 on the math-science literacy test, besting only Cyprus (446) and South Africa (356). The questionnaires accompanying the tests, however, turned up some interesting cultural factors that influenced the scores.

For instance, students were asked how many hours a day they worked at a paid job. In most countries, children are students only. But in the United States, fully 27% said they worked more than 3 hours a day at a job, and another 28% indicated they worked 5 or

TABLE 24.5   Rankings of 31 Countries' Reading Achievement for 4th Graders and 9th Graders, 1991

TABLE 24.5A Countries Ranked by 4th Grade Reading Achievement: Total Score

Country	Mean	Standard Error
Finland[a]	569	3.4
United States	547	2.8
Sweden[b]	539	2.8
France[c]	531	4.0
Italy[c]	529	4.3
New Zealand[c]	528	3.3
Norway[c]	524	2.6
Iceland[c*]	518	0.0
Hong Kong[c]	517	3.9
Singapore[c]	515	1.0
Switzerland[c]	511	2.7
Ireland[c]	509	3.6
Belgium (French)[c]	507	3.2
Greece[c]	504	3.7
Spain[c]	504	2.5
Germany (West)[c]	503	3.0
Canada (British Columbia)[c]	500	3.0
Germany (East)[c]	499	4.3
Hungary[c]	499	3.1
Slovenia[c]	498	2.6
Netherlands[c]	485	3.6
Cyprus[c]	481	2.3
Portugal[c]	478	3.6
Denmark[c]	475	3.5
Trinidad/Tobago[c]	451	3.4
Indonesia[c]	394	3.0
Venezuela[c]	383	3.4

SOURCE: Elley, Warwick B. *How in the World Do Students Read?* The Hague: International Association for the Evaluation of Educational Achievement.
NOTE: * Iceland tested all students, therefore no standard error was calculated.
a. Mean achievement higher than United States.
b. Mean achievement equal to United States.
c. Mean achievement lower than United States.

more hours a day. The research on the impact of working on school performance has generally found a curvilinear relationship. Those who work up to 20 hours a week get better grades than those who work more or who do not work at all.

This relationship shows up in the TIMSS data as well:

Less than 7 hours a week: 484

TABLE 24.5 Rankings of 31 Countries' Reading Achievement for 4th Graders and 9th Graders, 1991

TABLE 24.5B Countries Ranked by 9th-Grade Reading Achievement: Total Score

Country	Mean	Standard Error
Finland[a]	560	2.5
France[b]	549	4.3
Sweden[b]	546	2.5
New Zealand[b]	545	5.6
Hungary[b]	536	3.3
Iceland[b]	536	0.0
Switzerland[b]	536	3.2
Hong Kong[b]	535	3.7
United States	535	4.8
Singapore[b]	534	1.1
Slovenia[b]	532	2.3
Germany (East)[b]	526	3.5
Denmark[b]	525	2.1
Portugal[b]	523	3.1
Canada (British Columbia)[b]	522	3.0
Germany (West)[b]	522	4.4
Norway[c]	516	2.3
Italy[c]	515	3.4
Netherlands[b]	514	4.9
Ireland[c]	511	5.2
Greece[c]	509	2.9
Cyprus[c]	497	2.2
Spain[c]	490	2.5
Belgium (French)[c]	481	4.9
Trinidad/Tobago[c]	479	1.7
Thailand[c]**	477	6.2
Philippines[c]	430	3.9
Venezuela[c]	417	3.1
Nigeria[c]**	401	—***
Zimbabwe[c]	372	3.8
Botswana[c]	330	2.0

SOURCE: U.S. Department of Education, Office of Educational Research and Improvement. (1996). *Reading Literacy in the United States: Findings From the IEA Reading Literacy Study.*
NOTES: ** Sampling response rate of schools below 80%.
*** Insufficient data to calculate standard error.
a. Mean achievement higher than United States.
b. Mean achievement equal to United States.
c. Mean achievement lower than United States.

7-14 hours a week: 506

21-35 hours a week: 474

More than 35 hours a week: 448

The score of 506 for those who work a moderate amount of time each week is slightly above the international average of 500, and the 484 is not far below it. Thus, those Americans who are most like the European peers in terms of time spent at a job come out as average. They have not fallen farther behind (to write this, of course, we have to assume that the international average is meaningful, something that probably isn't true).

The influence of cultural variables such as work week usually cannot be determined unless something looks peculiar in the data. For instance, in the First International Adult Literacy Survey (FIALS), most American immigrants scored at the two lowest levels and few scored at the highest. This alone makes it difficult to compare nations, because only Germany comes close to having the proportion of immigrants found in the United States. Beyond this, though, there is the peculiarity that while a substantial proportion of Canadian immigrants score at the lowest level, a substantial proportion also score at the highest levels (Organization for Economic Cooperation and Development, 1995).

In fact, a higher proportion of Canadian immigrants than Canadian natives scored at the highest levels. This outcome occurs because of Canadian immigration policy. Canada has a relatively open door, especially for relatives of people already in Canada. It also has an aggressive policy of recruiting highly skilled, well-educated people in other countries to come live in the land of the maple leaf. Such people usually have children who do well on academic tests.

The discussion of the work week and immigration policy calls attention to the fact that the American vision of childhood, especially the teenage years, is quite different from that in many other countries. This vision includes not only jobs, but malls, dating, cars, extra-curricular activities, and other things that probably serve to lower high school test scores. We expect our children to gear up academically in college. According to foreign observers, they do. Some foreign observers have suggested that international comparisons should be extended to college; they have implied that American students would fare much better at that level.

In other nations, the high school years have a much tighter link to life after high school, and high performance has a much higher payoff. In nations like Japan and Korea, students work extremely hard because which college they go to is critically important. Kazuo Ishizaka (1998), director of Japan's Global Education Institute, has written that, "In Japan, people tend to judge people not by what they know and can do, but by what school they have gone to" (p. 25).

Most Americans are familiar with the phrase *exam hell,* which describes what Japanese high schoolers go through, but Paul George's book, *The Japanese Secondary School: A Closer Look* suggests that this phrase fails to capture the pure torture of the senior year (George, 1995).

Few Americans would wish such an experience on their children. And, as Ken Schooland (1989) has observed, the sorting process backfires to some extent. Once the students are *in* college, they tend to go into an intellectual hibernation. Schooland found that they partied, drank, skipped class, talked when they were there, and cheated openly on tests. He was instructed to give passing grades to anyone who showed up with some degree of regularity.

We should note that the American approach to secondary education works well for only about 57% of all students. Some 65% of high school graduates go on to college for at least some time. Factoring in dropouts, this amounts to about 57% of all students. Kids who slough their way through high school and don't go on to some institution of higher education do not have a chance to recover from their unrigorous ways.

There were further aberrations in the TIMSS final year results. In the advanced mathematics test in TIMSS, 23% of the items assumed that students had taken a calculus course. Half of our students had not. They were in a precalculus class. They scored 100 points lower than American students who actually had calculus under their belts. That means that if we assumed that American students who had taken calculus scored at the 50th percentile, the precalculus students would be at the 16th percentile.

Actually, the American kids with calculus were very close to the average. The international average was 501. American students with calculus scored 492. Again, there is no evidence for some kind of achievement decline during high school where students have similar curricular experiences.

It must also be said that there are some very peculiar results in the final year report. For instance, students from Cyprus were 19th of 26 nations in the fourth grade, 37th of 41 in the eighth grade, and 20th of 21 on the final year math-science literacy test. These results certainly seem to imply that the longer Cypriot students stay in school, the farther behind their international peers they fall. Yet they were 6th in the advanced math test and, within that test, number 1 in the world in calculus. How is such an outcome possible? No one has ever put forth an explanation (See Bracey, 1998b, 1998c, and especially, 2000 for in-depth critiques of the TIMSS Final Year Report).

Part of any explanation would lie in who was tested. For the math-science literacy test, nations were supposed to draw representative samples. They were permitted to choose the testees for the advanced math and physics tests. In some instances this meant assessing a tiny elite. It is also the case that most nations do not have the culture of public self-criticism that is found in the United States. Saying negative things about the country and its inhabitants in public can result in jail, torture, or death. It could be that nations chose samples that they thought would make them look good.

In sum, there is little evidence that staying in school puts students at risk of falling behind their peers in other countries. What evidence there is implies a need for curriculum reform at the middle school level and implicates a host of cultural and societal factors at the secondary level.

CHAPTER 25

Why Are Test Scores Falling?

Short answer: They aren't.

The myth of falling test scores is pervasive. The sense of decline is heightened by the prevalence of misguided nostalgia and know-nothing-kid comments. Even when people *know better* they still succumb to the myth. For instance, the very first "Bracey Report on the Condition of Public Education"[1] grew out of an essay by *Washington Post* columnist Richard Cohen. I spoke with Cohen several times on the phone and he encouraged me to submit a version of my analysis to the *Post*. I did, and they ran it in their Sunday Outlook section (Bracey, 1991a). During the construction of the "Second Bracey Report" (Bracey, 1992), I had occasion to speak with Cohen on the phone again. He appeared sympathetic and also appeared to understand what I was saying. Yet, in his column of August 4, 1992, Cohen wrote that during the Reagan/Bush years "the country got . . . dumber on just about every achievement test the kids could take" (p. A19).

In all honesty, a number of school critics have acknowledged that scores are rising. The new lament—for we can never express any satisfaction—from these reformers, though, is that the achievement of the schools has risen a little but the demands of the workforce have risen a lot. Ergo, things are still in an awful state. This damning-with-faint-praise message, though, has yet to reach the general public or much of the media.

For most tests, we do not have long-term trend data. For many years, commercial achievement tests were tests with no fixed standard. When each new renorming was carried out, the median raw score became the 50th percentile (the national norm), whatever that raw score turned out to be. And it varied. Once, while director of research and evaluation for Cherry Creek (Colorado) Schools, I was confronted with a decision in choosing what norms to apply to our test scores. We had been using 1985 norms, but Riverside Publishing had come out with 1989 norms. Using 1985 norms would provide continuity and let us look at trends; using 1989 norms would give us results compared against more current national results.

We decided to do both. Actually, when the results came in, Riverside had applied four sets of norms to the data, those from 1979, 1982, 1985, and 1989. Each newer set of norms was more difficult, indicating that achievement was rising in the nation. That is, the same raw score that converted to, say, the 65th percentile with the 1979 norms would fall to the 62nd using 1982, 59th using 1985, and 56th using 1989. Another way of saying this is that students had to get more items right in 1989 to get the same percentile rank as in 1985, the 1985 students had to get more items right to get the same percentile as in 1982, and the 1979 students had the easiest time of all attaining a given percentile.

There are two exceptions to this floating-standard problem, the SAT and the "Iowas," the Iowa Testing Programs—the Iowa Tests of Basic Skills (ITBS) and the Iowa Tests of Educational Development (ITED). By Iowa law, each new version of these tests must be equated to earlier versions, providing a continuity of scale not available from other tests. The scores for the ITBS are shown in Figure 25.1 (H. D. Hoover, personal communication, March 1999). ITED scores showed the same trend up to 1992, but at that time the scale for the ITED was changed, rendering more recent scores not fully comparable to earlier scores. We can observe, however, that there has been no tendency to this point in time for the ITED to decline from the year that the new scale was first used. That is, even though we can't see the full trends for the ITED, we can observe that there has been no fall since the new scale was introduced.

The ITBS trend lines *for Iowa* show that from 1955 to roughly 1965, scores rose. Then, for about a decade, they fell. As noted in Part I, this was quite a decade. It began with the Watts riots in Los Angeles, and these were followed over a period of years by disturbances in virtually every major city. It was a decade that contained Vietnam and the anti-war protests, Watergate, Kent State, SDS, the

Figure 25.1. Achievement Trends for Iowa, Grades 3-8, on ITBS Test C

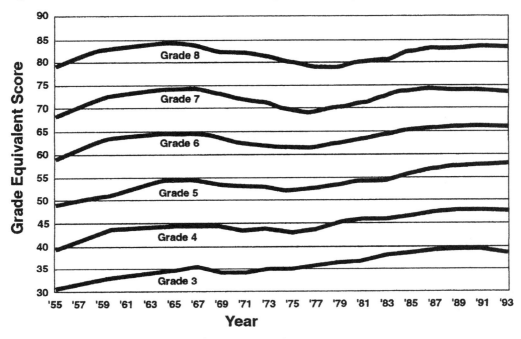

SOURCE: H. D. Hoover, University of Iowa (personal communication)

Black Panthers, women's rights movements, the civil rights move-ment, the Summer of Love, Woodstock and Altamont, and the as-sassinations of Martin Luther King, Jr., and Robert F. Kennedy, Jr. The panel convened by the College Board to examine the fall in SAT scores called it a "decade of distraction." It was certainly that.

A popular song of the day said of Vietnam, "Ain't no time to wonder why, whoopee we're all gonna die." It seems probable that during such a period, people were paying less attention to factoring equations and parsing sentences (at least until they got to college and needed the "2S" deferment to avoid the war).

But about the same time that the last American helicopter took off from the roof of the American Embassy in Saigon, test scores started up again (the year varies a little by grade).

By the mid- to late 1980s, most grades had reached *record highs.* In recent years, scores in Iowa have started to fall. To repeat that, Figure 25.1 presents the trends over time in Iowa. That is impor-tant. Iowa differs from many states in two ways: Its demographics

Figure 25.2. ITBS Average Composite Scores for Iowa (1962-1990)

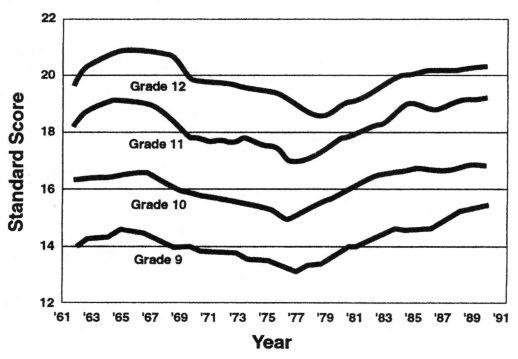

SOURCE: H. D. Hoover, University of Iowa (personal communication)

have only recently begun to change (see below), and the Iowa tests have been around since the 1930s. Iowa remains an agricultural state with no large cities (Des Moines, twice as large as any other urban area, has a population of about 250,000).

Moreover, the Iowa Testing Program is a voluntary program although virtually everyone participates. It is not, however, a high-stakes program. No one's bonus, promotion, firing, retention in grade, graduation, or selection into special programs depends on the results. To see if data actually supported the contention that the tests are not high stakes, H. D. Hoover, who directs the Iowa Testing Program out of the University of Iowa, once compared the percentiles of Iowa students on the ITBS to their percentiles on NAEP (National Assessment of Educational Progress). No one, of course, would argue that NAEP was a high-stakes testing program.[2] The students' ranks on both tests were virtually identical.

Figure 25.2 shows ITBS scores for Iowa through the most recent renorming. The national trends track the Iowa trends very closely, indicating that they are not just a Midwest phenomenon.

The ITBS is currently being renormed, and the results should be known sometime in early 2000. This is a matter of some interest as the interpretation of the decline in Iowa varies. Program director H. D. Hoover thinks—he says it's no more than his opinion—that teachers are spending too much time caring for kids' self-esteem.

I think the decline might be due to a change in demographics. As noted in Chapter 17, "Beware of Changing Demographics," the frozen demographics of Iowa are thawing and most of those moving into Iowa—Bosnians, Mexicans, Hmong—are not native English speakers.

The trends shown in Figures 25.1 and 25.2 are for the composite score. When I looked at the changes in the subtests, I found at least weak evidence for changes in instructional focus and for language problems. Reading scores, for instance, are down. That could be a change induced by demographic changes. Math computation scores are down, but math problem-solving scores are up. On the surface, at least, that looks like a change in instructional emphasis. It will be interesting to see what the results of the national norming sample look like.

National norms using scores from districts that use the ITBS have remain flat at the record levels. There is some question that the districts that actually use a test, though, have the same representativeness as those that were recruited for the national norming sample. The "user norms"—norms from districts that actually use the tests—are flat at all-time highs, but scores in Iowa have declined for about 3 years.

It is more difficult to render precise statements from SAT trends. While the "recentering" (the same thing as a renorming of an achievement test) of 1996 altered the scale, it did not disrupt our ability to look at trend data from the SAT—ETS (Educational Testing Service) and the College Board have conversion tables that allow one to go back and forth between the old scale and the new.

What makes definitive statements difficult about the SAT is— changing demographics. The test-taking pool is a self-selecting one made up of high school seniors who want to attend colleges that require the SAT. That pool has grown in size over the past four decades. In 1960, only 30% of high school seniors took the SAT. Currently, it's about 45%.

The original standards for the SAT were set in 1941. The onset of World War II interrupted the administration of the essay section of the test, and the College Board later decided simply to move ahead with nothing but multiple choice questions. In 1941, the average score was assigned a scaled score of 500 and the standard deviation of the SAT was set to 100.[3] These standard setters probably didn't really represent the typical college student of the time and they certainly did not represent the current pool of SAT testtakers. The standard setters consisted of 10,654 students mostly living in the Northeast and mostly planning to attend Ivy League, Seven Sisters, and other private institutions in that region. Ninety-eight percent of them were white and 61% were male. Forty-one percent had attended private, college preparatory high schools. Currently, the pool consists of 52% female, 33% minority, and 83% public school students. Many also come from low-income families. In view of these demographic changes, the recentering makes good sense, as a score of 500 on the old scale in no way represents the typical college applicant at the end of the century.

The original SAT had a verbal and a quantitative section. The quantitative section quickly fell from an average score of 500 to about 475 by 1950 and was stable at that point until the infamous decline that began in 1963 and continued to 1980. No one has ever investigated this early decline, probably because many of the explanatory devices—family decline, television, drugs—are not available.

In 1963, the two scales began a 17-year decline. In 1976, the College Board convened a panel to examine the reasons for the fall. It's complicated, said the panel. It's simple, said the media and the public: High schools are failing. The panel concluded that most of the decline from 1963 to 1970 was occasioned by demographic shifts—more women, more minorities, more kids with mediocre high school records. It held, though, that changes after 1970 had to be due to other factors, as these three changes stabilized (the panel's staff of statistical analysts did not concur). It called the end of the first period of decline and all of the second a "decade of distraction" and mentioned some of the factors discussed above in connection with the decline of the Iowa tests.

In fact, the panel mentioned more. One of the background papers for the panel simply listed the hypotheses that had been brought forward by someone or another to explain the decline. There were 79 of them, mostly plausible on their faces.

Both scales reached a perigee in 1980. The "quantitative" section, now called "math," rose until 1985, leveled off until 1991, then headed up again. The verbal section rose until 1985, then fell until 1994, bottoming out at an all-time low in that year, before resuming an upward slope.

Demographics continued and continue to affect the scores. Scores in 1990 were lower than in 1975. In *Perspectives on Education in America* (Carson, Huelskamp, & Woodall, 1993), more commonly known simply as the Sandia Report, Sandia engineers showed that if the academic composition in 1975 and 1990 had been the same, scores would have risen. The composition over that period, however, contained more and more students with GPAs that placed them in the bottom 40% of their classes.

We can note that this last trend has various possible interpretations. It could be that the college curriculum was getting watered down. In the 1940s, educators had contended that no more than 20% of any senior class could cope with college-level material. It could be that colleges were maintaining their standards but seeking to increase revenues, creating more programs and adding students. Or, it could be a continuation of early civil rights initiatives in which low-income and minority students who had not done well in high school were afforded opportunities to attend institutions of higher education. Or it could be any combination.

Finally, in connection with the rise or fall of test scores, NAEP scores have generally been inching upward. This is especially true in the years since *A Nation at Risk*. That document was one of the most successful pieces of propaganda ever published. Its statistics were slanted and selective, its rhetoric overheated. And it was not long after it appeared that alternatives to public education began to grow in popularity. If public education in the United States meets its demise, dating it from *Risk* will not be inappropriate (Campbell, Voelkl, & Donahue, 1997).

In the short term, though, *risk* did have one benefit: Although students were already beginning to take more of the rigorous courses than they had in the 1960s, *Risk* accelerated this trend. This increased course taking, especially in math and science, is likely the cause for the increases in NAEP science and math scores seen since *Risk* appeared. The gains in math and science are shown in Figures 25.3 and 25.4.

The reader might notice what appears to be a contradiction in these graphs. The gains for each of the three ethnic groups are greater than the gain for everyone taken together. For example, in

Figure 25.3. Achievement Trends for National Norming Samples, Grades 3-8, on ITBS Test C (Composite)

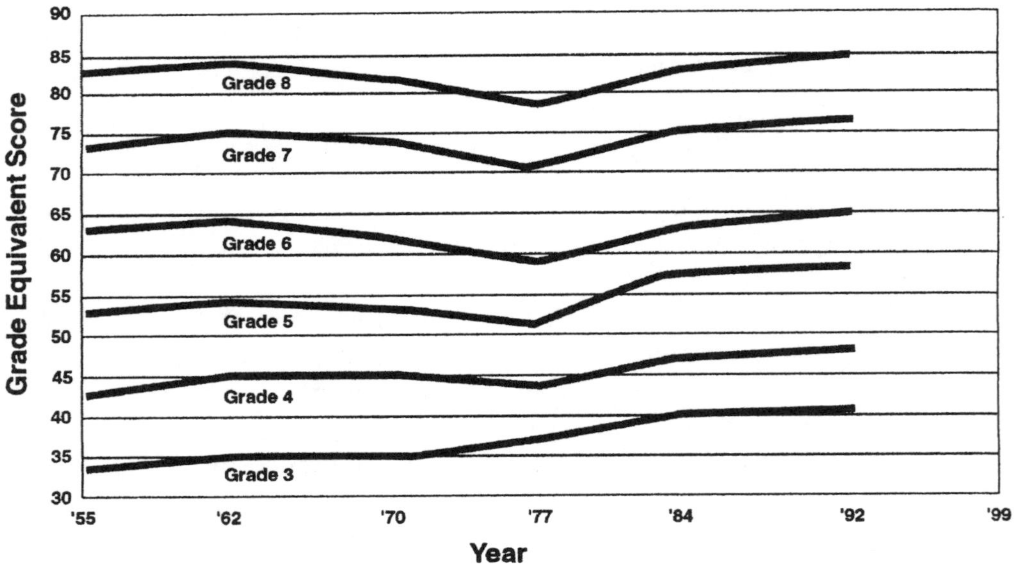

SOURCE: H. D. Hoover, University of Iowa (personal communication)

science the scores of whites, blacks, and Hispanics increased by 13, 22, and 12 points, respectively, but the overall average rises only 11 points, from 283 to 284.

This apparent contradiction occurs so often in research it has a name, Simpson's Paradox. A similar paradoxical trend was found by the Sandia Engineers for the SAT: Even though the trend for SAT scores was stable for whites and upward for other groups, the overall average declined.

The explanation of the paradox is that at the two different points in time, there were three groups of NAEP testtakers, white, black, and Hispanic (Asians had not yet become a large enough proportion of the population to establish a reliable estimate of their scores). But although the same three groups are present both times, they constitute different proportions of the whole sample at the two times. In 1996, blacks and Hispanics were a larger part of the sample. Their scores are improving, but they are still lower than the scores of white students. Thus, adding more of these low-but-improving scores tempers the overall gain.

Figure 25.4. Achievement Trends for Iowa, Grades 3-8, on ITBS Test C (Composite)

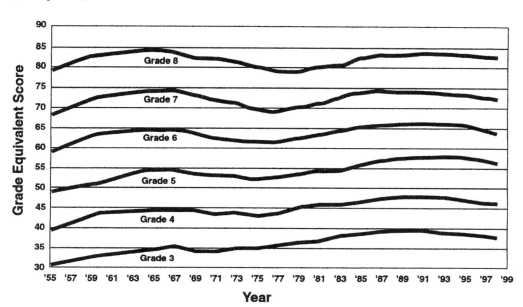

SOURCE: H. D. Hoover, University of Iowa (personal communication)

Because Simpson's Paradox affects test trends whenever demographics are changing, it is worth taking time to illustrate the paradox with an example. Consider the two sets of scores in Table 25.1.

Assume that in the left column, the 500s are the SAT scores of white students and the 400s are SAT scores of minority students. Together they give an average of 490.

Now assume that all of the 510s in the right column are SAT scores of white students and the 430s are the SAT scores of minorities. White students have improved by 10. Minority students have improved even more, by 30 points. Yet the average has fallen from 490 to 486. This is because minority students are only 10% of the group in the left column but 30% of the group in the right column.

The goal, of course, is not only to get everybody's score up, but to close the gap. In the meantime, we need to be aware that a falling average that is due to the changing composition of the group is a different phenomenon than a falling average due to everybody getting dumber.

TABLE 25.1   SAT Scores and Simpson's Paradox

500	510
500	510
500	510
500	510
500	510
500	510
500	510
500	430
500	430
400	430
490	486 (average scores)

A corollary to the contention that scores are falling is that the proportion of students who do obtain high scores is also falling. This argument has been made both for the SAT and for NAEP.

In the fall 1998 issue of *The Concord Review*, Stephan Thernstrom, professor of history at Harvard and author, with his wife Abigail, of *America in Black and White*, clucked over the state of American education. We quote extensively because his opening words are exemplars of the statements that lead people to think test scores are skidding:

> It is hard not to feel discouraged about the state of our elementary and secondary schools these days. We spend more and more money on education each year, but what we have to show for the investment is very much open to question. For more than a quarter century now, the National Assessment of Educational Progress has been monitoring the achievement of representative samples of American students at the ages of nine, thirteen, and seventeen. The results are disheartening. At the end of their high school education, our students today are not significantly better at reading, writing, or math than they were a generation ago, and their command of science is discernably weaker.
>
> The performance of our very best students has been particularly depressing. In every subject, the scores required to make it into the top decile and the top 5 percent are lower than they were in the early 1970s. (Thernstrom, 1998)

TABLE 25.2   Scores for 17-Year-Olds

Mathematics	*1978*	*1996*
90th percentile	344.7	345.6
95th percentile	355.7	354.7

Science	*1977*	*1996*
90th percentile	346.2	351.7
95th percentile	361.5	365.3

Reading	*1971*	*1996*
90th percentile	341.7	340.4
95th percentile	356.5	354.4

Are you depressed yet? Not surprising.

It is not clear what Thernstrom's reference point is. His opening sentence mentions both elementary and secondary schools. He then shifts to high school seniors only, and his comment on the top 5% and 10% of our students has no specification at all.

Let's take a worst case scenario and see what the picture looks like for only 17-year-olds (Table 25.2). So . . . Are we to assume that the Winthrop Professor of History at Harvard University cannot read tables? Did he forget? Or did he see the results he wanted to? As we see here, in any case three of the salient scores are "higher" and three are "lower." I put these words in quotes, of course, because who on earth besides professor Thernstrom would call any of these differences meaningfully large? Even the 4- or 5-point gain in science would not be considered a lot, although it might be statistically significant given the huge sample sizes.

But professor Thernstrom has said that the "command of science is discernably weaker." What he must be referring to here are the average scores over time. In 1970, the average score for 17-year-olds was estimated to be 305 (estimated because at that time NAEP was not constructed to provide trend data; attempts were made to extrapolate backwards in time from the 1977 assessment). In 1996, 17-year-olds scored 296 on NAEP science.

Does a 9-point difference over a 26-year period reflect a command of science that is "discernably weaker"? By what criterion? The 1996 score is statistically significantly lower than the

1970 extrapolated score. Without further information we cannot say more than that.

Alas, Professor Thernstrom has been done in by Simpson's Paradox. Blacks and Hispanics constitute an increasing proportion of the NAEP sample. Indeed, when the first NAEP reading test was given in 1971, Hispanics did not constitute a sufficiently large group to show up as a separate category in the NAEP report by ethnicity. NAEP scores for blacks and Hispanics have been increasing, but they are still below those of white students. As blacks and Hispanics have come to constitute a larger portion of the low, their improving-but-still-lower scores have served to attenuate the overall average, just as Simpson's Paradox predicts.

When we look at the 90th and 95th percentiles by age and by ethnicity, of the 54 relevant comparisons (three ages, by three ethnicities, by three subjects, by two scores), only two are down. They both show up in the 18 comparisons that pertain only to 17-year-olds. Over a 25-year span, the 95th percentile for white students declined from 358.9 to 358.4. The 95th percentile for white students in mathematics fell from 357.8 in 1978 to 357.7 in 1996, a stunning free fall of one tenth of one point.

In fact, NAEP scores rise for all three ethnicities at all levels of performance, not just the upper level (95th percentile). When we look at the lower performers (5th percentile) and average performers (50th percentile), we find their scores showing healthy upward trends. Sometimes the gains are dramatic. For instance, the 5th percentile for black 17-year-olds is now 35 points higher than it was 28 years ago. On the NAEP scale, 28 points is a lot. Their average scores are up 26 points, and the 95th percentile for black 17-year-olds is fully 20 points ahead of where it was in 1971.

NOTES

1. This article was actually titled "Why Can't They Be Like We Were?" (Bracey, 1991b). I had no intention at the time of writing a series on the topic.

2. Or, at least, would have when Hoover made his comparisons in the early 1990s. As NAEP has become more visible and used in part for bragging rights among states, questions have arisen about the validity of the changes in scores in some states.

3. These numbers are arbitrary. The procedure for creating scaled scores is quite straightforward, involving subtracting each score from the average score and dividing by the standard deviation. This creates a scale with a mean of zero and a standard deviation of 1.0. Adding a constant or multiplying by a constant does not alter the relationship of the numbers. Multiplying by 100 and then adding 500 gives a scale with a mean of 500 and a standard deviation of 100. A number of other scales of the day had means of 50 and standard deviations of 10 or means of 100 and standard deviations of 15 (e.g., IQ tests). The College Board was looking for a scale that could not be confused with other scales. It succeeded. It did, however, create a scale that makes small differences look large. For instance, a gain on the SAT of 15 points, say from 500 to 515 moves a person only from the 50th percentile to the 56th. A gain of 15 points on an IQ test would take a person from the 50th percentile to the 84th.

CHAPTER 26

How Come Private Schools Do so Much Better Than Public Schools?

Short answer: They do?

This is a hard question to answer decisively because public and private schools differ on so many variables. There are the "old line elite" schools like Andover and Choate. There are segregationist academies formed to resist racial integration. There are traditional Catholic schools, and within this group there are schools that are primarily academic and others that see their primary mission as establishing the Catholic religion in students. There are also the new privates set up to turn a profit.

Occasionally a private school will claim superiority by comparing its test scores to those of the public district in which it resides. This begs the question, of course, unless the private school shows that its demographics are similar to those of the district as a whole. On average, private schools are favored by affluent families and those with higher levels of education.

New charter schools will likely make the same claim. Here another set of data would be even more appropriate—and even less likely to be revealed. Since many if not all of the charter school students attended public schools in earlier grades, we should look at those scores in comparison to the scores in charter schools. Have they increased, decreased, or stayed the same?

TABLE 26.1   NAEP Scores for Reading, Math, and Science

Math

Age	Public	Private	Difference
9	230	239	9
13	273	286	9
17	306	316	10

Reading

Age	Public	Private	Difference
9	210	227	17
13	257	274	17
17	286	294	8

Science

Age	Public	Private	Difference
9	229	238	9
13	255	268	13
17	295	303	8

NOTE: These are data for ages 9, 13, and 17 taken from *1996 NAEP Trends in Academic Progress*. Data from the individual NAEP "Report Cards" (O'Sullivan, Reese, & Mazzeo, 1997) for each subject report out in grades, not ages. In addition, some of the newer Report Cards use different scales that are not comparable across time or across grades and any given point in time.

Given the affluence and educational levels of private school parents, one must wonder why private schools don't outscore public schools more than they do. The raw results of average scores from NAEP (National Assessment of Educational Progress) reading, math, and science are shown in Table 26.1.

For the most part, these are not large differences, and the largest difference, in reading, diminishes over time. Students in private schools show no more growth over time than students in public schools. This suggests that the differences in private and public schools stem more from different starting points than from differences in the quality of education.

Occasionally it is alleged that because of their greater holding power, the private schools suffer at the upper age. Dropouts from public schools presumably take their lower test scores with them. Data from one table in the *1996 NAEP Science Report Card*

TABLE 26.2   Science Scores by Type of School and Level of Achievement

	Percentile				
	10th	*25th*	*50th*	*75th*	*90th*
Grade 4					
Public	103	127	151	172	188
Private	126	145	165	182	197
Grade 8					
Public	102	126	151	172	191
Private	123	143	164	182	199
Grade 12					
Public	103	126	151	174	192
Private	115	136	156	175	191

(O'Sullivan, Reese, & Mazzeo, 1997), though, give more credence to the different starting points hypothesis (unfortunately, each NAEP assessment is a separate contract, and the report cards do not contain precisely the same analyses. It would be interesting to see this data set for reading and mathematics). These data (Table 26.2) show test scores at different grades and at different levels of achievement. Scores are shown for the 10th, 25th, 50th, 75th, and 90th percentiles.

The largest differences between public and private schools occur at the youngest age and lowest percentile. Students at the 10th percentile in the fourth grade of private schools score 23 points higher than their public school peers. The fourth-grade 90th percentiles are only 9 points apart. This likely reflects the "open-door" policies of public schools and the ability of private schools to select students.

For all three grades, the average score-difference (50th percentile) is smaller than the difference at the 10th percentile.

The difference also diminishes over time, and it is this that gives the different-starting-points contention greatest credibility. The 10th percentiles are 23 points apart at the 4th grade, 21 points apart at the 8th grade, and 12 points apart at the 12th grade.

Scores for public and private schools converge as age and performance grows. Thus, the 75th and 90th percentiles at the 12th grade reveal no differences between public and private schools.

NOTE: It is possible, but unnecessary, to separate Catholic from "Other Private Schools." The two types of schools score at virtually the same level. For 13 of the 15 comparisons, the differences between Catholic schools and other privates are 3 points or fewer. Sometimes the difference favors Catholic schools, sometimes it favors other private schools. The two larger differences occur at the 10th percentile and are 5 and 7 points, both favoring Catholic Schools.

An earlier analysis of NAEP data by Albert Shanker and Bella Rosenberg (1992) of the American Federation of Teachers found that there were small differences favoring private schools when the parents either had not completed high school or were high school graduates. For parents with some postsecondary work and for parents who were college graduates, the scores of the children were virtually identical.

As noted earlier, the educational level of parents who use public and private schools is different. Shanker and Rosenberg also found that 18% of public school parents had at least 4 years of college. The figure for Catholic and private nonsectarian schools were 30% and 57%, respectively. When education levels and affluence levels are factored out statistically, differences between the achievement of public and private schools disappear.

In the past couple of years, a lot of propaganda has been put forth about the "magic" of Catholic schools. An article in the January 25, 1999, *Investor's Business Daily* was actually headlined "The Magic of Catholic Schools" (Chapman, 1999). Earlier, former Assistant Secretary of Education Diane Ravitch (1996) asked in *Forbes,* "Why Do Catholic Schools Succeed?"

Some of the paeans to Catholic schools are easily dismissed. In a "Backgrounder" from the Heritage Foundation, Nina Shokraii (1997) wrote,

> Opponents of school choice often state that Catholic schools succeed because they can pick and choose students, they have more freedom to dismiss disruptive students, and their parents are more involved in their children's education. The evidence, however, proves otherwise. According to Lydia Harris, principal of St. Adalbert, a leading Catholic school in Cleveland, "There's no cream on my crop until we put it there. It's a myth that we take discipline problems and throw them out of school. It's the other way around. I get the kids the public schools can't handle."

Anyone willing to accept the above quote as "the evidence," is likely to find happiness in a field other than research.

Ravitch observes that in public schools, 84% of the students whose parents have a college degree take geometry, but only 59% of those whose parents did not graduate college do so. In Catholic schools the figures are 91% and 92%, respectively. "Across the curriculum, the same pattern emerges: the public schools allow students to choose easy courses, while the Catholic schools have the same high expectations for all their students" (Ravitch, 1996, p. 81). As noted above, one study found that 18% of public school parents had at least a bachelor's degree, compared with 30% of Catholic school parents.

With the additional education and the increased proportion of students taking math, one must then ask why the differences in NAEP mathematics scores between public and private school students are so small. For the most recent NAEP assessment, the difference at the 12th-grade level was 8 NAEP scale points, an average of 303 versus 311. In science, the difference for the 12th-grade average score was even smaller, 155 versus 151.

An interesting qualitative look at the differences between public and private schools was undertaken by Richard Rothstein of the Economic Policy Institute, Martin Carnoy of Stanford University, and Richard Benveniste of The World Bank (Rothstein, Carnoy, & Benveniste, 1999). These researchers approached the different types of schools to test six hypotheses about the differences derived from cliches one often hears:

1. Private schools are more accountable to parents.
2. Private schools have more clearly defined outcomes and expectations for students.
3. Private schools have better behaved kids with a better set of values.
4. Private schools have more efficient teacher selection and retention practices.
5. Private schools obtain their success with the same kinds of curriculum used in public schools (at least, for common subjects).
6. Private school innovations stimulate improved practices at the public schools with which they compete.

The researchers found no support for *any* of these hypotheses. The most accountable schools were public schools in affluent areas. In at least one school, parent input was so overwhelming that the school set up a panel to review parents' questions and criticisms. The panel published a weekly newsletter about them. One teacher reported that she got a letter a week from every one of her kids' parents with specific curricular suggestions; another said that 25 parents showed up on the first day of school to tell her how to organize the curriculum. Well-educated, affluent public school parents said they had "a right" to participate in their children's education. Not exactly the "Berlin Wall of Educational Monopoly" (see Chapter 27 for an explanation of the origins of this phrase).

Affluent private schools were responsive, too, but their administrators were more successful at convincing parents that curricular and instructional matters were entirely the prerogative of the school and its teachers and administrators.

Low-income schools, both private and public, struggled to make the *parents* accountable and responsive. Administrators in these schools "complained frequently that too few parents volunteered in classrooms, that too few parents attended meetings to discuss school policy or to review children's work, and that parents paid insufficient attention to the importance of homework" (Rothstein et al., 1999, p. 6). One teacher reported making one phone call a week to the parents of students who were doing very well or doing poorly, but not receiving much in the way of constructive responses. Private schools were more successful here because they could make participation a condition of admission, but most of the involvement was in fund-raising endeavors.

Where parents in low-income public schools did become involved, it was more likely to be to challenge disciplinary decisions. At some schools where passivity prevailed on curricular or instructional issues, the faculty were often challenged on disciplinary matters (a situation made more difficult by large differences among teachers in what was considered acceptable behavior).

In one private, for-profit school studied, accountability consisted of a warning: "Caveat emptor." The school had been in existence for 28 years before any kind of parent advisory group was formed. Even now, it refuses to distribute rosters of students' names and phone numbers. The school claims it is to protect privacy. In fact, it is to keep parents from communicating with each other.

The reader is referred to the paper, "Can Public Schools Learn From the Private, Non-Profit Education Sector?" for a rewarding discussion of findings relative to the other five hypotheses (Rothstein et al., 1999).

CHAPTER 27

Why Don't We Have Vouchers so the Money Would Follow the Child?

Short answer: Because vouchers have been tried elsewhere and have failed. They have produced all of the bad outcomes that voucher critics predicted. The results from small-scale experiments with vouchers in this country are small, if they exist at all, and in any case, could not be generalized to the larger system.

It *is* true that vouchers have been tried elsewhere; we will be discussing the case of Chile later on. But that outcome has to date been irrelevant to the relative absence of vouchers in this country. To date, voucher experiments have been just that, experiments. They have operated on a small scale, and even if they were successful, they have been conducted in a tiny arena that is so different from schooling as a whole that it is doubtful that the findings of the experiments could be generalized to the nation or even to an entire large school system.

The theory behind a voucher system contends that competition in a market-driven school system produces better results. Good schools would be rewarded with more students and bad schools would go out of business. This would lead to a much better system than our current "monopolistic" public school system. At a conference on privatization in September 1998, the present system was referred to as "The Berlin Wall of Educational Monopoly." This is a silly statement, as those in attendance, almost all of them voucher advocates, acknowledge that people who can afford to choose where they live have a powerful de facto school choice available to them. In fact, that is one reason why voucher initiatives have failed: The people who are most likely to vote are most likely to be satisfied with their schools and have not supported voucher referenda.

In spite of an absence of positive data, the conference, cosponsored by two Texas right-wing organizations, the Children's Educational Opportunity Foundation and the National Center for Policy Analysis, served as the forum for some engorged rhetoric about choice. Perennial candidate Lamar Alexander led off his talk with, "There is a vast left-wing conspiracy to deprive poor children of a good education. Rarely has such a grand army as our own held the high moral ground for so long and advanced so little." Alexander offered no explanation for why the grand army had made so little progress.

The conference itself was devoid of the data from the various experiments. The Milwaukee experiment was mentioned, but as a court case, not a research problem (the person who mentioned it was Clint Bolick, who had recently successfully argued the case for the defendants before the Wisconsin Supreme Court; the U.S. Supreme court declined to hear the case). The peculiar way the "results" from this study entered the culture was discussed in Chapter 1. Here we expand that discussion.

In 1991, the Milwaukee legislature approved the use of public money to provide students with vouchers to let them attend private, nonsectarian schools. Initially, the program was limited to 1% of the total public school enrollment, and only those with incomes at or below 175% of the official U.S. poverty line were permitted to apply. In 1993, the program was expanded to 1.5% of the school population, and in 1995 the law was changed to permit the vouchers to be used at church-related schools, and it was the suit over this expansion that Bolick had argued. Also in 1995, the Wisconsin Supreme Court ruled that the private schools participating in the program did not have to gather the achievement data required for the comprehensive evaluation specified in the law. Thus, while there were annual evaluation reports through the school year 1994-1995, there have been no meaningful evaluations of the program since then.

The evaluations conducted through 1995 found no differences between the voucher students and a control group of Milwaukee public school (MPS) students. Differences among the groups and statistical peculiarities afflicted the evaluations from the beginning. Parents of the students in the program were found to have more education and higher expectations for their children's academic careers than the MPS control group. The proportions of parents in all groups who returned surveys were small.

As noted in Chapter 2, Jedi Warrior Paul Peterson found that after 4 years, students in the choice program scored higher on tests of reading and math. Reanalyses by Cecilia Rouse (1998) of Princeton University were able to replicate Peterson's results for math, but not for reading. In addition, when she used scores for the same children for more than 1 year, the effect disappeared entirely.

Looking at Milwaukee public schools that had small classes and low-income students, Rouse found these schools to outperform the voucher schools. In addition, she found that the voucher schools actually had the smallest classes of all. Thus, *if* students in the choice program show improved achievement, small classes is a better explanatory variable than is some magical choice effect.

Most of the voucher programs in this country are too new for a summative judgment. To date, most have shown little in the way of gains. In one instance where the gains were large, the researchers admitted that they could not disentangle the effects of selection from the effects of program (Hill, Foster, & Gendler, 1990). That is, the students who entered private schools with vouchers might have done well because of the excellent program they received or they might have done well because they were already doing well.

In the spring of 1999, at the behest of Governor Jeb Bush, the Florida legislature passed a law that provides vouchers to students who attend schools that receive an "F" from the state's grading system. This is the first large-scale voucher system in this country. It will be interesting to see what happens. It will be interesting to see how the program is evaluated, if it is, by the state.

In the meantime, voucher critics can take heart from the study of vouchers in Chile. In 1980, the Pinochet regime transferred control of schools from the ministry of education to localities. At the same time, it put in place a Milton Friedman-inspired plan to have schools compensated based on enrollment. Private schools could participate in the system as long as they did not charge tuition over and above the value of the voucher.

In the ensuing period, the percentage of students attending elite private schools that do charge tuition has varied consistently in the

5% to 9% range. By 1998, however, almost 40% of Chilean students were enrolled in what Stanford University researchers Patrick McEwan and Martin Carnoy (1999) refer to as "commercial" schools. Some of these are new schools, often started by former public school principals. Some are existing schools that received partial subsidies under the old system.

Carnoy and McEwan gathered test scores and socioeconomic information about the students in the various schools. According to Carnoy and McEwan (1999),

> Vouchers in Chile have not produced the educational results proponents claim for them nor what the poor might have expected. For example, our analysis of nationwide test score results from 1983 to 1997 shows that pupils in most of Chile's private subsidized (voucher) schools do not outperform public school pupils once socio-economic background differences are accounted for. Instead, vouchers redistribute pupils with better educated parents from public to private schools. Nor has the competition made public schools better. School improvement in Chile came mainly from a centralized, reformist bureaucracy intent on improving the least successful schools, not from free-market competition. (p. 1)

The scores of public schools have improved. At first glance this could be taken as the result of a free market operating according to theory. After all, the competition for pupils is supposed to cause lower-achieving schools to work harder. Unfortunately for the theory, scores rose more in municipalities that had only public schools. That is, in communities where there was no competition. Carnoy (personal communication, June 29, 1999) advises that the government obtained improvements with some physical fixups, but mostly with new curriculum materials and a lot of teacher in-service training.

Parents appear to be choosing private schools more for status reasons than because the schools are perceived as academically superior. Even though public schools have smaller classes than the private ones, better educated, higher-SES parents tend to opt for the private schools where their children can attend school with the "right" peer group. Principals in private schools also entice parents with pitches about their ability to get students into the better secondary schools and the low-cost public universities. Admission to both of these latter institutions is highly competitive.

Why Don't We Use
Charter Schools as
Laboratories for Innovation
for the Rest of the System?

Short Answer: Because it's not clear that charter schools will be laboratories for innovation even for themselves, and because it flies in the face of the long history of school change.

We must separate this question into two smaller components: What are charter schools and what are they accomplishing? What does this mean for the rest of us?

Albert Shanker, the late president of the American Federation of Teachers, popularized the concept of charter schools. Shanker proposed that a school be granted a "charter" that would waive many of the allegedly onerous rules, regulations, guidelines, and procedures that the district as a whole followed. In return for the resulting autonomy, the school promised to increase achievement.

The idea appealed to many people, including those who advocated market-based choice programs and those who opposed choice. The proponents of choice saw charter schools as a step in the right direction. The antagonists saw them as less threatening, probably because so many of them operated with some clear oversight from some public agency—school board, university, state education agency, or even the district within which the charter school resided. And some people advocated charters simply because they thought diversity in schools was itself a good thing.

From the beginning, however, this apparently simple principle was compromised by reality. In the first place, in spite of the promise of accountability, few charters or districts or states established procedures to determine whether the promise of increased achievement had been kept. As early as 1994, Jeffrey Henig of George Washington University observed that charters "show few signs of interest in systematic, empirical research that is ultimately needed if we are going to be able to separate bold claims from proven performance. Premature claims of success, reliance on anecdotal and unreliable evidence are still the rule of the day" (p. 234).

Two years later, three ardent supporters of charters, Chester E. Finn, Jr., Lou Ann Bierlein, and Bruno V. Manno (1996), echoed Henig's lament:

> We have yet to see a single state with a thoughtful and well-formed plan for evaluating its charter school program. Perhaps this is not surprising, given the sorry condition of most state standards-assessment-accountability-evaluation systems generally. The problem, however, is apt to be particularly acute for charter schools, where the whole point is to deliver better results in return for greater freedom. (p. 7)

About the same time, Alex Molnar (1996), perhaps with a perspective from the Performance Contracting debacle of 20 years earlier, looked at the conditions that depressed Henig and the rest and predicted that,

> Charter schools will fail, fraud will be uncovered, and tax dollars will be wasted. But just as certainly, glowing testimony will be paid to the dedication and sacrifice of the self-less teachers and administrators at some "Chartermetoo" school who transformed the lives of their students and proved the success of charter school reform.
>
> Free-market zealots will either claim vindication or argue that their revolutionary ideas need more time to work. Supporters of public education will call the experiment a costly failure and marvel at the willingness to spend large sums on unproven alternatives while cutting resources for the public system that serves most children. With an absence of any uniform

standards, the war of educational anecdotes will remain "subject to interpretation." And all the while, the desperation of America's poorest children and their families will grow. (p. 167)

Four years later, pretty much everything that Molnar had predicted would happen has happened, along with some other things as well. As is so often the case, the reality of education is more complex than the theory.

In fairness, not all charters were established with a promise of increased achievement, at least the kinds of achievement that show up on standardized tests. Some have been designed to provide students with an "Afro-centric" curriculum, or with an environment where students can learn English without at the same time learning that Spanish is bad. In addition, I have some real questions about the charter-granting agencies' approvals.

For instance, a number of charters have been granted to people who have never run a school before, but who had some kind of vision for what a good school should look like. These people have discovered that running a school involves a lot of very hard work and calls for skills they might not have. Not everyone can establish and monitor a budget, procure supplies, obtain facilities or a grant to build them, or negotiate with the fractious demands of multiple constituencies. Most people have never written the kinds of goals and outcomes statements that those calling for accountability would like to see. In the up-to-my-ass-in-alligators situation that they find themselves, it is not unreasonable for them to overlook the draining-the-swamp activities of establishing standards and measurement systems.

In at least one state, this inexperience has produced a disturbing trend. In its evaluation of charter schools in Michigan, Western Michigan University found that the number of charters operated by private concerns has risen from 50% in 1997 to 70% in 1978 (Horn & Miron, 1999). "It was a real burnout situation," said one charter school founder as she turned the school over to a private, for-profit company. This is disturbing because the private sector schools often come with prescribed curricula and frown on any deviance from that curriculum. This stifles the kind of creativity and innovation that energized the charter school movement in the first place.

There are other disturbing trends as well. In Arizona, for instance, the charter schools have a much higher proportion of white students than do the public schools that are physically closest to them (Cobb & Glass, 1998). The Western Michigan University evaluation of Michigan charters noted that, "In relation to the host districts, the charters as a whole have fewer minorities. Thus there is support for those who argue that the charter schools are skimming and increasing segregation" (Horn & Miron, 1999, p. 17).

More disturbing is the situation in Arizona where the state has formally backed away from evaluating charter schools. Initially, the State Department of Public Instruction had an evaluation team headed by an assistant superintendent to check on what was happening in the schools. The team started turning up problems. According to the Arizona *Tribune,* "while the monitors were supposed to focus on whether schools were complying with laws and charters, those with education backgrounds found it hard to ignore such things as out-of-control classrooms or the absence of instruction" (Todd et al., August 24, 1998, p. 1). Thomas Toch, education writer for *U.S. News & World Report,* observed a school where faculty are paid bonuses for rising enrollments. He found one class of 30 students sitting through a course called "American Literature Through Cinema." When Toch visited, the class was studying *The Last of the Mohicans.* Except that they weren't watching it, they were merely listening to the soundtrack. At least, notes Toch, those who were still awake (Toch, 1998).

The evaluation team in Arizona also found instances where some "high schools" were using materials suitable for middle school and "teaching" two and three shifts of students a day. This is possible because Arizona law requires high school students to attend class 4 hours a day. Toch's conclusion from his experiences in Arizona and Michigan was that, "What is clear from the Arizona and Michigan experiences with charters is that without rigorous accountability, both students and taxpayers suffer."

Other studies have concluded that such charter school accountability is lacking. Amy Stuart Wells (1998) of UCLA led a team of researchers in an evaluation of California charters and concluded that, "It is not clear that charter schools are being held responsible for anything more than the public schools are held to, although in areas where they have more control over resources, they sometimes have to report their use of these resources in more detail" (p. 24).

That is, charter schools lose their charters when they mismanage money, not when they mismanage learning.

As noted, not too much attention is being paid to increasing achievement. And, where achievement is rising, it might not be due to the dynamics of "charterness"—it might not be ascribable to the new autonomy and flexibility the charters are based on. For instance, the evaluation of charters in Michigan observed that 37% of them contained fewer than 100 students, and fully 61% contained fewer than 200. Only 9% of regular Michigan public schools are this small. Although direct evidence is lacking, many people feel that small schools produce better results. And direct evidence that does exist clearly indicates that small classes do.

For some charter school advocates, the innovations of the charter schools themselves are just the beginning. The important changes will occur—according to theory—in the larger system. For instance, Ted Kolderie (1995) once wrote:

> Too often, those asking "what's happening?" [in regard to the impact of charter school laws] look only at the schools created and the students enrolled: the first-order effects of a law. There are also second-order effects: changes/responses in the main-line system when laws are enacted and schools created. An evaluation needs to look for these. . . . Despite what the words seem to imply, "charter schools" is not basically about the schools. For the teachers who found them, and the students who enroll in them, true, it is the schools that are important. But for others, from the beginning, "charter schools" has been about system reform, a way for the state to cause the system to improve. The schools are instrumental. (p. 5)

If the schools themselves are only instrumental, then one must say that, to date, they haven't generated much music in the larger system. One study found the districts "had gone about business as usual and responded to charters slowly and in small ways" (Rofes, 1998). Other evaluations have found similar inattention to the charters (Horn & Miron, 1999; Wells, 1998).

Perhaps the system changes will come later, after the charters are established and their innovations more widely known. But perhaps not. Most evaluations to date have not found charters exploring new avenues of curriculum and pedagogy:

In summary, there are many opportunities for charter schools to learn about innovative practices. Since all of these schools are newly developed with the exception of the relatively few converted private or parochial schools, one might expect that innovative practices would be frequent and widespread. However, such is not the case. We found unpredictably few innovations, which would not suggest that transportability is an immediate expectation. In fact, we found the charter schools to be remarkably similar to the regular public schools. (Horn & Miron, 1999, p. 77)

CHAPTER 29

Why Are We Throwing
Money at Schools?

Short Answer: Are we?

Naturally, one must further define "throwing money at."

In some instances, these words are translated as "the United States spends more money on its schools than any other nation." This is not true, nor has it ever been. It is true that among Organization for Economic Cooperation and Development (OECD) countries, the United States ranks second in per-pupil expenditure for elementary schools and third for secondary schools. But it is also true that schools in the United States provide many more services than schools in most other nations (Organization for Economic Cooperation and Development, 1996, 1998).

The United States is the only country with more nonteachers than teachers in the schools. In some countries, such as Belgium and Japan, the teaching force constitutes close to 90% of all school personnel. Is this evidence of the "administrative blob" that has been alleged to suffocate education? Not at all.

According to the 1998 *Digest of Education Statistics,* the proportion of administrators in schools shrank from 2.6% in 1950 to 1.6% in 1996, while the proportion of principals and assistant principals declined from 3.3% to 2.4%. The proportion of teachers in schools also declined in this period, from 70.3% to 52.1%. On the other hand, instructional aides increased from 1.7% to 10.1%, and support staff went up from 23.3% to 31.0%. Most of this shift occurred by 1980, and the relative proportions have been pretty stable for the past 20 years (p. 90).

The allegation that we are "throwing money at the schools" comes from two different kinds of analyses, both flawed. One looks at the correlation between state-level per-pupil expenditures and various state-level outcomes. The other looks at the change in spending over time at the national level and the change in NAEP scores over the same period.

The source of the first analysis is former Secretary of Education William Bennett, via the American Legislation Exchange Council (ALEC), a conservative think tank. This "analysis" was discussed in Chapter 2 under the principle "Follow the Money." To repeat, Bennett observed that some states with high SAT scores did not spend a lot of money on schools and some states with low SAT scores did. Bennett did not take into account the differing SAT participation rates among different states.

Brian Powell and Lala Carr Steelman (1996) analyzed the state-level SAT scores, statistically factoring out the differences in participation rates. They found that most of the differences among states were explained by the differences in participation rates. They also found that for every $1,000 above the national average a state spent for education, total SAT scores, so tenuously connected to the classroom, rose by 15 points.

Howard Wainer (1993) at ETS (Educational Testing Service) also challenged Bennett's analysis. Statistically correct for differential participation rates, Wainer analyzed state-level results for the National Assessment of Educational Progress (NAEP). The SAT testtaking pool is self-selecting, and the proportion of students involved varies enormously from state to state. NAEP, on the other hand, always selects a representative sample of students. Wainer observed a clear relationship between money spent and NAEP scores.

Eric Hanushek is the principal source of the other kind of analysis. In 1989, Hanushek declared that "there is no strong or systematic relationship between money and achievement." Given Hanushek's primitive statistical technique, it would have been impossible to find either a "strong" or a "systematic" relationship. Hanushek used a "vote counting" procedure: If a study showed a positive and significant relationship, that category got a vote. If it showed a positive but not significant relationship, it got a vote in that category. Such counting could never reveal strong or systematic relationships. Still, Keith Baker (1991) promptly pointed out that Hanushek's own data contradicted his conclusion: There were far more studies in the positive count than one would expect if there were truly no relationship (Baker, 1991).

Hanushek has persisted both in using the vote-counting methodology and on insisting that money doesn't matter. His usual contention turns on increases in spending coupled with "flat" NAEP scores. Since even the aggregate NAEP scores have been rising in recent years, it is hard to see how he can continue to use them to support his contentions. And, as shown in Chapter 25, the aggregate NAEP scores mask increases, sometimes dramatic increases, in the scores for different ethnic groups.

Hanushek has also refused to acknowledge those studies that contradict his conclusion. Some of the studies that have been included in his analyses are, at the very least, of questionable relevance.

A recent study indicates that both school funding and level of poverty affect school performance (Payne & Biddle, 1999). Using data from the Second International Mathematics Study and census data, Payne and Biddle found that, "If American math achievement scores had been generated only by well-funded schools in districts with low levels of poverty, the United States would have scored slightly better than the second-ranked nation in the study, the Netherlands" (p. 11). By contrast, if Payne and Biddle had used only low-funded schools in high-poverty districts, we would have fallen close to the ranks occupied by Nigeria and Swaziland.

The study also found something that we are number 1 in: child poverty among industrialized nations. The United States has 21.5% of its kids in poverty, with poverty defined as 50% of the median income of all persons. No one else even comes close. Australia is second with 14.0%. Curiously, five of the top six countries in poverty rates are Anglophone: the United States, Australia, Canada, Ireland, and the United Kingdom, in that order. David Berliner contends that this is a legacy of British mercantilism in which the exploitation of children is acceptable (Berliner, 1999). Israel places fifth. Payne and Biddle (1999) are more than just a little angry about the situation:

> Surely it is time to put to rest the absurd myth that level of funding does not matter for public schools in America. Rich American parents have known otherwise for years, hence their willingness to provide well-funded public (and private) schools for their own children in affluent neighborhoods. It is long since time that parents from middle-class and disadvantaged

homes woke up and demanded well funded schools also be made available for *their* sons and daughters. (p. 12)

It is possible, of course, for schools, as with any organization, to waste money, to spend it in ways that do not lead to improved education (at least, improved in terms of rising test scores). The saga of Kansas City schools appears to be a case in point (Ciotti, 1998). Kansas City decided that the way to improve the test scores of its mostly black population was to have them sit next to white kids, most of whom were living in the suburbs. A federal judge refused to force the suburbs into consolidation, but encouraged the lawyer for the plaintiffs who brought the consolidation suit to "dream" about what they might want in a school district that would lure suburban students back. Kansas City spent huge sums on what can only be called a "Field of Dreams" strategy—build it and they will come. Its budget rose from $125 million per year in 1985 to $432 million in 1992.

The district built beautiful schools and stocked them with courses in garment design, ceramics, violin, drama, and foreign languages. It built athletic facilities that would make colleges swoon. The fencing team took field trips to Senegal and Mexico. Administrators bought everything in sight: The accounting staff was overwhelmed trying to process 12,000 purchase orders a month.

Of course, it didn't work. KC expected to round up between 5,000 and 10,000 white suburban students. It got, at most, 1,500, and most of them went back to their neighborhood schools after one year.

There were problems in the system other than just spending money on noninstructional goodies. Many teachers were judged incompetent, even by the lawyer for the plaintiffs, who acknowledged that 20% were totally incompetent and another 20% needed retraining. But it was impossible to remove them. Teaching jobs were among the best paying in Kansas City. Black clergy, concerned about community job loss, made it difficult to fire them. Schools were seen as a jobs program, not as educational institutions. Unable to fire teachers, the district simply raised salaries for everyone by 40%. This apparently did nothing to lure new teachers into the system, but it cemented the old ones in place.

The system suffered other indignities. It was hard to find people to run for the school board. According to a report on the issue, most of those on the board earned less than $30,000 a year at their jobs and had difficulty dealing with complex financial issues.

If it was hard to find competent board members, it was harder still to find people for the superintendency. The district churned through 10 of them in 9 years. People with national reputations took themselves out of the running once they actually met with the school board.

So the message is this: If you throw money at politically dysfunctional schools with incompetent teachers, administrators, and board members who are operating under a plan that has little to do with learning constructed by a naive lawyer and approved by an equally naive judge, it probably won't work. If you spend your money directly in the service of instruction, it probably will.

Most of the new money for schools since 1969 has *not* been spent in the service of instruction, at least instruction in regular classrooms. Since 1969, spending on special education grew by 425%, from 4% to 17% of the total budget. Special education received 38% of the new money, regular education less than a quarter (the rest went for targeted programs that would not be expected to result in rising test scores; Lanford & Wyckoff, 1995; Rothstein & Miles, 1995).

CHAPTER 30

Why Are SAT Scores
Still Falling?

In short: They aren't.

The overall average SAT scores reached their lowest point in 1980 and 1981 at 502 for the verbal and 492 for the math (all scores presented here use the 1996 recentered scale). In 1999, the verbal average was 505 and the math was 511. However, the proportion of seniors taking the SAT has been continually increasing. With the SAT average representing an ever-deeper dig into the talent pool, one might well have expected the average to decline.

The average has not declined and, once again, the overall averages mask changes for the various ethnic groups. Starting with the low year of 1981 and using total scores for simplicity of the table, we obtain the following results:

1981	1999	
1,029	1,055	White
799	856	Black
1,011	1,058	Asian
928	965	American Indian
899	909	Mexican American
868	903	Puerto Rican

NOTE: The College Board has recently added a category to cover other Latin Americans. Over the decade for which data are available, 1989 to 1999, Latino scores dropped from 932 to 927.

As noted in the section on "Watch for Selectivity" (see Chapter 4), the proportion of high scorers on the SAT math has grown substantially in this period. The proportion grew 75% from 1981 to 1995, after which the figure cannot be calculated because of recentering. The proportion of high scorers on the verbal has also been edging up, although it is nowhere near its high point.

About 5 years ago I predicted that the SAT verbal would continue to fall because we were moving much more into a multimedia, iconic culture. That has not come to pass. It might be due to the increase in rigor of course taking in high school.

31

Why Don't Bright People Go Into Teaching?

Short answer: Teachers hold their own compared to people in other professions.

One possible answer could be this: "Teaching is so tough an occupation and pays so middling wages that no bright person in their right mind would do it." William Glasser (1990) once estimated that teaching was so subtle an art that no one could do it for more than 2 hours a day: "What parents, administrators, school board members, politicians, education reporters, and teacher educators misunderstand is that being an effective teacher may be the most difficult of all jobs in our society" (p. 429).

Fortunately, there are people who are willing to commit themselves to this difficult chore, and those who do, hold their own intellectually, at least on tests.

The myth that people who go into teaching are not very bright has been around for many years, and for most of that time it hung on a slim thread of indirect evidence: High school seniors who said that they were going to major in education had lower SAT scores than those indicating an intent to major in most—not all—other subjects. In addition, who knows what high school seniors actually declared as majors at the end of the sophomore year (and, for some, again in the junior and senior years).

This datum was also confounded with gender. Most teachers are women and, as a group, women score lower on the SAT than men. The difference is small in the verbal section, substantial in the math. A study by the Educational Testing Service, though, showed that despite this difference, women got higher grades in freshman college math whether that math was the regular freshman offering, calculus, advanced algebra, or some other advanced course. Women taking remedial math had the same grades as men. Since there were some 45,000 people in the study, the higher grades likely cannot be attributed to the women being "cute" (Wainer & Steinberg, 1992).

Ironically, a study that was intended to *prove* that teachers are less able ended up showing the opposite and, as a consequence, ended up getting buried in the bowels of the U.S. Department of Education (Lee, 1984). The study was commissioned shortly after *A Nation at Risk* appeared in 1983. When people looked for scapegoats for the "dreadful" state of our schools, teachers were a natural target. Some people thought the problem had gotten worse over the past decade: While the average SAT score had fallen for almost 20 consecutive years, SATs for future teachers fell more.

Using data from a very large database, the Cooperative Institutional Research Program at UCLA, John Lee of JBL Associates examined the grade point averages (GPAs) of those who said they would major in education, those who said they would major in a subject and teach, and those who said they would major in a subject and enter a profession other than teaching. The grade point averages examined were both those of the students as high school students and at the end of the college sophomore year—that is, before education majors started taking those "gut" Ed School courses.

The high school GPAs of those who said they would teach did not differ from those who intended other majors and other professions. Nor did their GPAs fall between 1974 and 1983, the period studied. Those who said that they would major in a subject and teach had consistently lower GPAs than those naming similar majors, but the differences were tiny, .01 to .05 of a point.

As college sophomores, those who planned to teach had a GPA of 2.88, while those majoring in a subject averaged 2.87. By their senior year, the teacher candidates' GPA had risen to 3.08, those of other majors to 2.95. That is, there were no differences, and few indications of "grade inflation."

The questions that differentiated teacher prospects from other majors were the reasons given for the major. Teachers were not particularly interested in job availability considerations or money. A much larger proportion of other majors considered job availability

(44% vs. 20%) and financial prospects (33% vs. 6%) as factors in determining their major subject.

The people who commissioned the study were not pleased. On the phone, researcher Lee said, "We made one presentation to the Department [of Education]. It didn't go over too well with the political appointees."

So, if the study got quashed, how did I find it? Purely by accident. It was mentioned in my presence by David Imig, of the American Association of Colleges for Teacher Education. Imig was amused at the study's entombment. I thought he ought to have been outraged. I badgered him about the author until his memory found John Lee. Fortunately, Lee remembered that the Department of Education program officer for the study, Daniel Morrisey, had managed to slip the study into the ERIC system before the Department disappeared it.

Recently, a new study corroborated Lee's results, this time comparing the performance of actual teachers with people in other professions. Barbara Bruschi and Richard Coley of Educational Testing Service analyzed data from the National Adult Literacy Survey (NALS) by profession (Bruschi & Coley, 1999). NALS produced literacy results on a scale similar to that of NAEP. The researchers then collapsed that scale into a scale of 1 to 5 with 5 being the highest level. NALS reading assessments are not "See Spot Run" type materials. They are drawn in many instances from actual passages an adult might encounter in the real world. The passages are difficult, sufficiently difficult that even people who score at the lowest levels trying to cope with them still report that they read newspapers and magazines. They also report that reading difficulties are not an impediment in their everyday lives.

NALS produces different scales for prose literacy, document literacy, and quantitative literacy. Although these are no doubt highly correlated, differences in proficiency do appear for different groups. Prose literacy includes interpreting instructions, inferring themes from poems, and understanding opinions in editorials. Document literacy required people to cope with job applications, payroll forms, schedules, maps, tables, and graphs. Quantitative literacy required not only reading but the manipulation of numbers taken from text—balancing a checkbook, figuring out a tip, or determining an amount of interest from a loan advertisement.

For the three literacies, about 10% of teachers reached level 5, with another 75% at levels 3 and 4. This is much better than the general population. About half of the population scored at the lowest 2 levels. Depending on the type of literacy, between 9% and 15% of teachers also did so.

The proper comparison, though, is not of teachers with the general population but of teachers with others of similar education. Only about 25% of the populace has at least a bachelor's degree, while 100% of certified teachers do, and more than half of them have at least a master's. When teachers holding a bachelor's degree are compared with other adults with bachelor's degrees, the scores are virtually identical. These results also show up when teachers with graduate training are compared to others with post-college degrees.

Looking at teachers versus various specific professions, only systems analysts outscored teachers in prose literacy. Systems analysts and electrical engineers bested them in document literacy. These two professions, plus accountants and lawyers, outscored teachers in quantitative literacy. Teachers consistently outscored educational administrators in all three literacies, although none of the differences were statistically significant.

The researchers also compared the salaries of various professions. The teachers' high levels of literacy did translate into salaries comparable to those in other professions.

CHAPTER 32

With All This Talk About Standards and Accountability, Why Aren't Teachers and Administrators Held Accountable?

Short Answer: In many ways, they are.

We must acknowledge at the outset that it is far too difficult to remove incompetent teachers. Even the NEA and AFT have acknowledged this problem. Part of the problem is union rules. But part of it is also difficulty in finding a universal definition of teacher competence. I doubt that beyond a level of subject matter knowledge and some obvious attitudes about child development, we likely won't reach such a definition because I think good teaching is situational. Classes differ from year to year. Teachers differ from year to year and condition to condition.

A tale I once heard during a meeting of teachers:

A teacher recalled the time when his district hired a new science teacher who, for some reason, canceled at the last minute. The school distributed the science courses among other teachers and this man, a mathematics teacher, got physics. He recalled his anxiety all year at being just ahead of the students.

Then, 8 years later, a young man walked into the teacher's classroom and announced that he had been in that class. He also said he spite of that horrendous year. The student said it was *because* of it. He felt that the teacher, struggling through the material, had given an object lesson in what a good problem solver does when he doesn't know the answer. The teacher had provided an opportunity for students to see a mind at work, something that is usually reserved for only advanced graduate students (it is true that for many people a hallmark of intelligence is what a person does when a person doesn't know what to do. This capability usually goes under the name of "resourcefulness").

There are many questions unanswered by the story: Would the student have gotten his PhD in physics anyway? Did anyone else benefit in this way or were they frustrated that the teacher was not engaging in "chalk and talk" instruction? We can't know. But anecdotes about the one teacher that made all the difference are too frequent to be discounted. How does one devise an accountability system to capture these dynamics? As Richard Rothstein (1999) has noted, the fact that a student takes an Advanced Placement course as a senior might owe as much to his or her experience with the first-grade teacher as to the 11th-grade teacher.

Even in the first grade, students do not enter classrooms as blank slates. Holding the third-grade teacher accountable for each successive wave of her second graders is an iffy task. Tracy Kidder (1989) captured the flavor of classes and variation in classes well. In the course of spending a year in the classroom of a teacher named Chris, Kidder noted that Chris had found that

> This year's low math group wasn't like last year's, which was entirely remedial. It contained a gang of five boys, who, whenever she turned her back, threw snots and erasers and made armpit farts at the children who were trying to work, and among them was the boy who decided one day to start barking in class. Not, Chris knew, because of Tourette's Syndrome, some of whose victims bark involuntarily. This boy barked in order to get suspended so he'd have a holiday. (p. 35)

Such a rich description of the dynamics of classrooms leaves the abstract statistics of educational research drab by comparison. It is, of course, possible to look at things from different vantage points. The Earth looks different from an airplane than from ground level. Patterns can be seen from 35,000 feet that are not discernible at low levels. Still, given the richness of life in classrooms as described by

Kidder and other observers, abstractions like "education production functions," a favorite of economists, don't seem to have much meaning (in fact, education is so different from the transactions of commerce that one wonders about the utility of any applications drawn by analogy. There are those today who claim that education is just the provision of a service like any other. It isn't so.). After all, the patterns seen from a plane are naturally occurring events. Patterns created by statistical analyses are not, necessarily.

One approach to accountability that has received a great deal of attention lately is called "value added" accountability, one means of looking for patterns at places other than ground level. Developed largely by William Sanders at the University of Tennessee, the value added approach has received a great deal of press (Archer, 1999).

Using a large computer, Sanders identifies those teachers who are unusually effective at producing changes in students' test scores. To obtain this kind of information, each child has to be tested each year. Once, during research, Sanders divided teachers into five groups, from the most to least effective depending on their capacity to produce test score changes. Then he looked to see what happened to students who had three very test-effective or three very test-ineffective teachers in a row. In two districts with very different test scores, students with three consecutive test-effective teachers landed at the 83rd and 96th percentiles. Those with test-ineffective teachers were at the 29th and 44th percentiles (Sanders, 1998; University of Tennessee Value-Added Research and Assessment Center, 1997).

About these kinds of results, several things can be said:

1. The results are circular. Since the teachers are *defined* as effective or ineffective based on their previously seen capacity to produce test score changes, it isn't all that surprising to see them continue to do that.

2. Within the realm of circularity, the results are fairly impressive. It is at least a matter of considerable empirical interest to determine how the teachers accomplish their gains and what the teachers whose students show declining test scores are doing instead.

3. We don't know what the effective and ineffective teachers are doing as teachers. We do not yet have any corroborative evidence to demonstrate that these teachers are also judged as effective on criteria other than test scores. If you asked the principals or the parents

who the effective teachers are, would you get the same list? If not, how would you decide among the competing lists?

It is possible to have highly regarded schools and low test scores. The teachers at the Key School in Indianapolis don't impact test scores much, but they are not trying to. Their instruction, predicated on Howard Gardner's theory of multiple intelligences, involves a great deal of instruction that will never show up on test scores. Students at the Key School learn a foreign language, learn to play a musical instrument, and get daily lessons in art. Teachers teach "pods"—short courses on things that interest the teacher outside of school, like pottery making or Victorian architecture.

The vocabulary learned in music or Victorian architecture can never appear on a standardized test: It is too specialized. Knowing Spanish might help a student taking the SAT determine the meaning of an otherwise inscrutable word derived from Latin, but no such help will be forthcoming as students cope with the ITBS or other commercial achievement tests.

Indeed, when the state of Indiana put in place a test-based accountability system, Key School faculty faced a dilemma: give up what they thought was the right way to teach children or continue and incur some risk of losing accreditation. Their solution was to create many work sheets and drill exercises of the sort of skills seen on tests and to entice the parents to work on these sheets at home. Scores rose so much that the state sent over an inspector to make sure they weren't cheating.

4. Which brings us to the final observation: the value of the value-added is defined strictly in terms of test scores. If we were to put an accountability system in place based on value-added changes, we would be going against the accountability recommendations from Richard Rothstein that were mentioned in Chapter 12 under "Teacher (Principal, Superintendent, Board) Accountability," and that are discussed in more detail below. Rothstein, it will be recalled, argues that a district must spell out *everything* it thinks is important and base the accountability on changes in a composite index that reflects everything.

There are a few other observations we can make. It's not clear that the system is even feasible for everyone. One article noted that the calculations require at least one gigabyte of RAM. Most PCs these days come with 64 megabytes.

In addition, a value-added system like Sanders's would mean large increases in the testing budgets of most districts or states. The

In addition, a value-added system like Sanders's would mean large increases in the testing budgets of most districts or states. The system requires that every child be tested yearly in all subjects. Given the enormous testing requirements, it is unlikely that anything other than multiple-choice tests would be used. We noted earlier that in only a few situations, mostly limited to graduate school, do multiple-choice tests test anything other than low-level skills. And, by the law of WYTIWYG (Chapter 21), that means instruction will be aimed at low-level skills. And then there's Bracey's Paradox: Test scores mean something only when you don't pay any attention to them. Once you do, corrupting influences enter.

As might be expected, the Tennessee Value-Added Accountability System (TVAAS) promoters defend the use of multiple-choice tests:

> It is simply not true, as most test bashers claim, that multiple choice tests consist mainly of items that ask for the recall of facts. Anyone who doubts this statement should obtain a copy of the practice book for the ACT or SAT and work through one of the practice tests. Almost all the items require higher order thinking skills; almost none rely on factual recall. (Bratton, Horn, & Wright, 1997)

This statement is common enough among those who use multiple-choice tests to deserve a response. First, the contention that the SAT requires "higher-order thinking" has no basis in fact. Higher-order thinking is not defined, and without such a definition, the statement is meaningless. Second, revisit the description of higher-order thinking in Chapter 21. Recall that the SAT requires students to answer 85 verbal questions and solve 60 math problems in 3 hours. That doesn't leave too much time for higher-order thinking.

In fact, let's consider a couple of actual SAT items.

The analogies section contains analogies like this one:

Rib Cage:Lung:
1. skull:brain
2. appendix:organ
3. sock:foot
4. skelton:body
5. hair:scalp

If the product of five integers is negative,
At most how many of the five can be negative?

This requires you to *recall* that the product of two negative integers is positive and the product of a positive and negative is negative. From there is it simply serial multiplication to come to the answer that all five can be negative.

Or

$$X^2 + Y^2 = 0. \text{ What is the value of } 3x + 5y?$$

Any number multiplied by itself will be positive. The only way two positive numbers can sum to zero is if both are zero. Hence $3x + 5y = 0$. There's not much going beyond the information given here. In a speeded test like the SAT—there can't be.

If fact, in its advice on testtaking skills, the College Board offers this: "Keep Moving."

Even if the ACT and SAT required going beyond the information given, that statement on multiple-choice tests is disingenuous: The tests in Tennessee are not college admissions tests, they are fifth-grade and eighth-grade tests using items from commercial achievement tests.

The accountability system designed by Richard Rothstein (1999) for the Los Angeles Unified School District takes a much more balanced view and, one might say, thoughtful approach. First, says Rothstein, you have to figure out what you mean by achievement. He observes that in the days when Soviet Union shoe factories were graded only on the number of pairs produced, some of them took to making only small sizes. That way they made more pairs faster and with less leather, to boot. Similarly, if you define achievement only in terms of reading and math, people will concentrate their attention on those outcomes, ignoring or slighting others. Second, no matter how you define achievement, you have to consider the fact that schools account for only part of it. Third, measurement gets more difficult as the unit of analysis becomes smaller. It is easier to measure at the district level than the school level, easier at the school level than at the classroom level. Fourth, a proper accountability system is a long-term venture and expensive.

Considering these issues together, Rothstein lays out the system requirements:

> If a school system wishes to develop measurement indices for some aspects of student achievement, it should develop indices for all desired outcomes of the institution. Indicators reflecting each outcome should be weighted by their relative importance, creating a composite index of system performance. The institution should be held accountable for improvements in the composite score alone. The institution and/or its component units and employees should not be rewarded for improvements on only some indicators, even those of great importance, because of the danger that such an accountability system may establish incentives to improve some aspects of achievement at the expense of deterioration in others. (Rothstein, 1999)

Note that the system emphasizes progress, not some predetermined goal that might fail 98% of the schools, as, in fact, happened in Virginia. This is important, too, because schools will differ in the resources that kids bring to them: There is no way to isolate fully the effects of the school from those of the family and the community.

Weighting the indicators in the system "forces policy makers to confront the trade-offs that are inherent in the operation of any institution with multiple goals."

Among the indicators that Rothstein thinks we ought to consider in addition to the usual achievement measures: arts indicators, health indicators, history and social science indicators, parent involvement, freedom from violence, and elementary class size. A complex indicator that Rothstein thinks is important is adequacy of school facilities. Some possible elements of this indicator could be proportion of year-round classrooms with air conditioning, number of students housed in trailers or other irregular classrooms, percentage of schools without graffiti, and percentage with preventive maintenance performed on schedule.

In connection with the school facilities indicator, we can note that when it had a contract with Baltimore City Schools, Education Alternatives Incorporated painted and repaired the facilities and made them generally pleasant places to be. While achievement did not increase, the repairs improved attendance and community attitudes toward the schools.

We should note here, too, that while the school cannot be insulated from the family and the community, *gain* scores have been found to be much more insulated than scores for *level* of attainment. The most recent findings of this come from the testing data in Tennessee. The gains found there in reading, mathematics, science, and social studies were not correlated with either percentage of minority students or percentage of students on free and reduced-price lunch.

The Tennessee results are similar to those reported by Paul Barton and Richard Coley (1998) in *Growth in School*. This monograph examined changes in National Assessment of Educational Progress (NAEP) scores from fourth to eighth grade for a variety of groups, including different ethnic groups. In terms of levels, the rank order of the groups were white, American Indian, Hispanic, and black (Asians formed too small a group in the NAEP sampling design to be reported as a separate group). Whites scored about 40 points higher than blacks. However, all four ethnic groups gained about 50 points between Grades 4 and 8.[1] This, again, means that none of the gap between whites and minorities was closed, but neither were the minorities falling farther behind.

Is a gain of 50 points "the same" for all groups? This question presents an almost unanswerable problem from a developmental standpoint. It can be argued that a 50-point gain for blacks is *more* than a 50-point gain for whites because it represents a larger *percentage gain.* That is, in going from 192 to 242, black students grew by 26% from their score of 192 in the fourth grade. Whites, on the other hand, increased their score by 21%.

On the other hand, black students had more ground to cover, and one could argue that they covered less of the remaining part of the scale than did whites. Without some external criteria we cannot specify which is "more" or "more important," and we lack such criteria. For instance, if it were true that the growth shown by black students made it possible for them to succeed at, say, plane geometry, but that the growth for whites had no such payoff in terms of facilitating success in math courses, we could say that the black gains were more important. The NAEP scales are often portrayed by NAEP and NAGB (National Assessment Governing Board) officials as having this kind of criterion-referenced quality, but, in fact, they do not.

NOTE

1. This is not a "true" cohort study because the fourth graders and eighth graders are different people. However, the eighth-grade sample was drawn in the year that the fourth graders would have been eighth graders.

Conclusion

Let's begin summarizing the preceding analyses in terms of what they are not. They are not a call for complacency in school reform. I stress this because some people have grossly misinterpreted what the various "Bracey Reports" have said. For example, in a review of my book *Put to the Test,* David Gilman of Indiana State University accused me of making "attempts to demonstrate that all is well in public education" (Gilman, 1999). Later in the review Gilman claimed that I tried to "rationalize that there are no problems of note in U.S. schools."

In response to Gilman's assertions, I simply quoted from the conclusions of the Bracey reports from 1992 and 1993, respectively: "So let's get to work on the real problems—of education and society. There is certainly no dearth of them, nor are they small." "I repeat, as I have in earlier reports, that American schools face many challenges, some of them horrific. In this report I have detailed problems in the cities and alluded to the even more intractable problems in impoverished rural areas."

I do not understand Gilman's comments, as he appears to be wielding no ideological axe. But some do. I believe that their attempts to paint me as Pollyanna are an attempt to discredit all of my work. If I can be shown to wear only rose-colored glasses, I can easily be dismissed, because any fool can see that there are some real problems out there. For their efforts in *The Manufactured Crisis,* David Berliner and Bruce Biddle (1995) have received similar treatment, even though they went farther than I have in spelling out the details of real problems and offering solutions.

So, reader, even though this book has provided you facts for handling the tough questions, you have a lot of work to do. I truly believe, as I wrote in the "Ninth Bracey Report" (Bracey, 1999a), that there is a neurotic need to believe the worst about our schools. Schools are our most personally public institution. You can blame government for problems, but "government" is somehow remote. Schools are concrete, and their representatives walk among the local citizens every day. Ever since the end of World War II, schools have been blamed for social problems but have received no credit for the solutions. Sometimes neither credit nor blame is deserved. Schools were not why the Soviet Union got into space first. Nor were they the reason that 12 years later an American walked on the moon, something the Russians never accomplished. Schools did not produce the recession of the late 1980s, nor did they energize the recovery of the early 1990s. Even though pundits have of late been pronouncing another recession as "inevitable" but unpredictable, predictably, when it does happen, some will try to lay the blame at the schoolhouse door.

I can only urge persistence. When people say you're being defensive, say that these are the facts and that they are not being selected or spun. Invite your accuser to offer other facts. When people say you're just acting in your own self-interest, admit that, yes, it is in my self-interest to produce the facts. Invite your accuser to offer other facts. I am not aware of any major facts that are omitted from this book, and I have not tried to spin the contents. I do dismiss the Final Year part of TIMSS—and with good reason. I admit that test scores declined for about a decade. I admit that the SAT declined and claim only that its fall was due to many more factors than the simplistic interpreters have allowed for. What else is there? *A Nation at Risk* (National Commission on Excellence in Education, 1983) listed 13 indicators of risk. For 2 of these indicators, I have been able to find no data whatsoever. The rest are no longer true, if they ever were.

I urge persistence, because your first efforts are not likely to be met with success. I pelted *Newsweek* columnist Robert Samuelson with challenges to his derogatory comments for years before he finally wrote "Three Cheers for the Schools?" in which he admitted that the crisis rhetoric had been badly overblown. I pelted columnist David Broder with similar challenges, and while Broder has written nothing positive about the schools, he has become the dog that didn't bark—he has not written anything nasty for years.

One strategy I urge on readers is to get information about the *nation's* schools into the hands of your local constituents. A survey by the American Association of School Administrators (AASA) found that people get their information about the nation's schools largely from radio and television. But when asked where they got information about local schools, they cited mostly local sources. No doubt this contributes to the common finding that people think their local schools are OK and that the nation's schools are in crisis.

The important implication of the AASA survey, though, is that people will not see accurate information about the nation's schools unless someone sticks it into local newsletters or mentions it at board meetings or at parents' night. Consider putting some of the statistics given here and in *Setting the Record Straight* (Bracey, 1997) into your parents' newsletters. Perhaps you can put them into a format like the little statistics boxes used by *USA Today*.

Or maybe you will want to undertake something more ambitious and devote a flyer to some specific statistic. I recommend that you contact the Center on Education Policy and obtain its series "Did You Know?" These are one-page flyers devoted to a single "fact": So far (the Center and its publications are relatively new), the Center has published flyers on rising science achievement, rising math achievement, rising SAT scores, rising college attendance, and decreasing school violence. Even if you don't want to reproduce the entire flyer, it will provide conveniently copyable graphs about the statistic in question, not to mention useful information. The flyers published through late 1999 have been assembled into a booklet: "Did you Know . . . The Good News About American Education?" The booklet is published jointly by the Center and The American Youth Policy Forum, also in Washington, DC. The Center is at 1001 Connecticut Avenue, NW, Suite 619, Washington, D.C. 20036; phone, 202-822-8065; *www.ctredpol.org*.

And while you are handling the tough questions with the data provided in this book, acknowledge and deal honestly with real problems. The people I have watched put out smoke screens about the problems usually ended up choking on the gas themselves.

Hang in there.

A RESOURCE

POP QUIZ ANSWERS

1. The statistics on home schoolers and ACT scores raise the issues of selectivity and representativeness. Who gets schooled at home? Typically, these children are the offspring of people who are more affluent and better educated than the public at large. They are children who would do well on tests as long as they weren't locked up daily in a dark basement. We can't really tell if they are doing better than expected unless we can compare them with a demographically similar group of students in public schools. Even then, the comparisons would not be strictly proper: Home schoolers are in educational environments where the pupil-teacher ratio is usually 1:1. That *ought* to mean higher test scores.

Rhode Island students score high because only a tiny fraction of them take the ACT. About 70% of Rhode Island seniors take the SAT. Since SAT scores are accepted not only at Rhode Island colleges, but at all colleges in the Northeast, the Rhode Island students taking the SAT are students aiming for some out-of-state university, such as the University of Colorado or Brigham Young, that makes more use of the ACT.

We don't really know if Virginia students scored "so low." Not many Virginia students take the ACT, either. Because of this, Virginia students are typically above average on the ACT. The average score is not presented.

2. Saying that the Russian economy grew 14% gives us a rate, a percentage, not a number. The information provided does not tell us

where the Russian economy is starting from. A 14% rate is good, but given the stories of the low state of that economy, it might well not mean that a recovery is soon forthcoming.

We would need to see the Gross Domestic Product of the nation over a long period of time to know how well Russia is or is not doing (something that would be hard to obtain, communist nations having been notoriously secretive about such statistics).

3. The two SAT figures, 1,014 for all students and 964 for those saying they intend to major in education, come from high school seniors. It will be another 2 years before any of them actually declare a major, and some of those will change majors one or more times before graduation. And while it is generally known that 50% of those who enroll in college do not finish, we don't know if the attrition is higher for education majors than for those majoring in other fields.

Gross's statement presumes that all of those who declared an intent to major in education became teachers. It also presumes that those who announced an intention to major in something else did *not* become teachers. But both statements are known to be untrue. Many teachers, especially those headed for careers in secondary schools, major or minor in an academic field and also take enough education courses to qualify for accreditation.

The one study that compared future teachers with other majors found no difference in college grade point averages at the end of the sophomore year. The one teacher who compared actual teachers with people in other professions found teachers' reading skills exceeded by only a few, usually scientific, professions.

4. One wonders what constitutes "virtually every measure." Forty years ago from the time of Gross's speech would put us in 1959. This would be one year after *Life* magazine had run a five-part series on the "crisis" in education, a crisis signalled by the Soviet Union's launch of Sputnik. Still, it might well be that schools, especially secondary schools, did have lower test scores. The high school graduation rate at the time was approaching 70%, well below the 83% of today. Since those who leave high school do so primarily because they are having academic difficulties, these dropouts would presumably take their lower test scores with them.

The fact is, though, that "virtually every measure" amounts to virtually naught. What measures could we look at? Not the National Assessment of Educational Progress (NAEP). It hasn't even been proposed yet. Not the SAT. Although the use of the SAT was increasing rapidly, only 564,000 SATs were taken in 1959-1960, compared with 1,200,000 today. The precise statistics we need aren't lying around, but the 564,000 constitute only 30% of all high school *graduates*. Currently, about 43% of the *senior class* takes the SAT.

The only test scores we have that link the two time periods are from the Iowa Tests of Basic Skills and Iowa Tests of Educational Development. These tests indicate that performance was lower in 1959 than it is today. So the one measure we do have contradicts Gross. Beware of nostalgia.

5. This report raises the issue of the difference between statistical significance and practical significance. The students with the lower GPAs are earning almost $200 a month more than those with the highest GPAs. I expect that this latter group of students would find a $200 a month increase, a raise of almost 20%, to have some real practical significance for them.

One might wonder why students with low GPAs out-earn those who have at least a "B" average. We can only guess, because the report does not address the issue. My guess is that students with high grade point averages who are not in college probably disdain dirty work. I would imagine that a large percentage of them are moping around trying to "find" themselves since they are not doing what most of their academic peers are, attending college or some other postsecondary institution. Those with low grade points might well have taken hard jobs such as construction work that initially pay well but that offer few career opportunities.

6. This is as much a logical conundrum as anything else. If 80% of all cities are experiencing shortages of skilled labor, how can only 58% of them say it's affecting their ability to attract new business? On the flip side, if a business were to experience difficulty in finding skilled workers, where could it move to? It would have only 20% of American cities to choose from.

One can wonder, as well, how close the mayors are to this problem. Who benefits by saying that there is a shortage of skilled labor? The mayors. Who loses? By implication, the schools, since it is implicitly the schools' fault.

7. All of the above questions have been taken from very recent reports (as of this writing), most of them appearing in the popular press. This question and the next are drawn from the book itself. The comments of Will and Bennett draw us back to Principle 2, "Follow the Money." Who benefits from these comments? The political Right that wishes to contend that money is not important to school performance. And those who wish to indict many schools for wasting that money—New Jersey, it is implied, is wasting money because it spends more and gets less.

The statements also raise a question about the measure. Is the SAT, whose middle initial originally stood for "aptitude," the right criterion measure of "achievement"? The people who developed it certainly didn't think so. And is "dollars per student per year" the right measure of money spent? Certainly not without factoring out differences in buying power, which are quite large among states.

Bennett's statement, as noted earlier in the test, also raises the question of selectivity. Of the states named, only Minnesota has as much as 10% of its senior class taking the SAT. New Jersey had 76% of its seniors bubbling in answer sheets. As noted, when these differential participation rates are factored out, the test score differences among states become small.

8. With this question we come back once more to the issue of making sure we have the right instrument. The National Assessment of Educational Progress was not designed to monitor closely what goes on in classrooms. Students, especially 17-year-olds, do not take it seriously. One wonders what kinds of pretty designs show up on NAEP answer sheets.

In addition, Hanushek has neglected to take Simpson's Paradox into account. Gains in the aggregate average, which is what Hanushek presents, are smaller than gains for individual ethnic subgroups. Over the period Hanushek discusses, the scores for ethnic minorities have been rising, but the minorities have become a larger and larger proportion of the total sample.

References

Adelman, C. (1999). *Answers in the tool box: Academic intensity, attendance patterns, and bachelor's degree attainment.* Washington, DC: U.S. Department of Education, Office of Educational Research and Improvement.

Allowing choice. (1998, July 7). *Florida Times Union,* p. A10.

American Educational Research Association, American Psychological Association, and the National Council on Measurement in Education. (1985). *Standards for test use.* Washington, DC: Authors.

Archer, J. (1999, May 5). Sanders 101. *Education Week,* pp. 26-28.

Atkin, M. J., & Black, P. (1997, September). Policy perils of international comparisons: The TIMSS case. *Phi Delta Kappan, 79,* 22-28.

Baker, K. (1991). Yes, throw money at the schools. *Phi Delta Kappan, 4,* 628-630.

Baker, R. (1983, April 30). Beset by mediocrity. *New York Times,* p. A23.

Barton, P. E., & Coley, R. J. (1998). *Growth in school.* Princeton, NY: Educational Testing Service.

Beaton, A. E., Martin, M. O., Mullis, I. V. S., Gonzalez, E. J., Smith, T. A., & Kelly, D. L. (1996). *Science achievement in the middle school years.* Chestnut Hill, MA: Boston College.

Beaton, A. E., Mullis, I. V. S., Martin, M. O., Gonzalez, E. J., Kelly, D. L., & Smith, T. A. (1996). *Mathematics achievement in the middle school years.* Chestnut Hill, MA: Boston College.

Bell, T. A. (1988). *The thirteenth man.* New York: Free Press.

Bennett, W. (1993). *Report card on American education.* Washington, DC: American Legislative Exchange Council.

Berliner, D., & Biddle, B. (1995). *The manufactured crisis.* New York: Addison-Wesley.

Bestor, A. (1953). *Educational wastelands: The retreat from learning in public schools.* Champaign: University of Illinois Press.

Bracey, G. W. (1991a, May 12). The greatly exaggerated death of our schools. *Washington Post,* p. C1.

Bracey, G. W. (1991b, October). Why can't they be like we were [The first Bracey report]. *Phi Delta Kappan,* pp. 104-117.

Bracey, G. W. (1992, October). The second Bracey report on the condition of public education. *Phi Delta Kappan,* pp. 104-117.

Bracey, G. W. (1993, September 29). George Will's urban legend. *Education Week,* p. 29.

Bracey, G. W. (1995a). The fifth Bracey report on the condition of public education. *Phi Delta Kappan, 77,* 149-160.

Bracey, G. W. (1995b). *Final exam: A study of the perpetual scrutiny of American education.* Bloomington, IN: Agency for Instructional Technology.

Bracey, G. W. (1995c). Money does matter. *The School Administrator, 53,* 38-41.

Bracey, G. W. (1995d, December 22). U.S. students: Better than ever. *Washington Post,* p. A19.

Bracey, G. W. (1997). *Setting the record straight: Responses to misconceptions about public education in the United States.* Alexandria, VA: Association for Supervision and Curriculum Development.

Bracey, G. W. (1998a). *Put to the test: An educator's and consumer's guide to standardized tests.* Bloomington, IN: Phi Delta Kappa International.

Bracey, G. W. (1998b). "TIMSS," rhymes with "dims," as in "witted." *Phi Delta Kappan, 79,* 686-687.

Bracey, G. W. (1998c). Tinkering with TIMSS. *Phi Delta Kappan, 80,* 32-35.

Bracey, G. W. (1999a). The ninth Bracey report on the condition of public education. *Phi Delta Kappan, 81,* 147-168.

Bracey, G. W. (1999b, September 2). We crush children under unrealistic standardized tests. *USA Today,* p. 17A.

Bracey, G. W. (2000). The TIMSS final year study: A critique. *Educational Researcher,* in press.

Bratton, S. E., Jr., Horn, S. P., & Wright, S. P. (1997). *Using and interpreting Tennessee's value-added assessment system* [On-line]. Available: www.shearonforschools.com/documents/TVAAS.html

Bruschi, B., & Coley, R. (1999). *How teachers compare: The prose, document and quantitative skills of America's teachers.* Princeton, NJ: Educational Testing Service.

Campbell, J. R., Voelkl, K. E., & Donahue, P. L. (1997). *Trends in academic progress.* Washington, DC: U.S. Department of Education, Office of Educational Research and Improvement.

Carnoy, M., & McEwan, P. (1999). *Public-private school differences in Chile's full-choice, marketized education system.* Unpublished manuscript, Stanford University.

Carson, C. C., Huelskamp, R. M., & Woodall, T. D. (1993). Perspectives on education in America. *Journal of Educational Research, 86,* 259-310.

Chapman, M. (1999, January 1). The magic of Catholic schools. *Investor's Business Daily,* p. 25.

Ciotti, P. (1998). *Money and school performance* (March). Washington, DC: Cato Institute.

Cobb, C., & Glass, G. V. (1998). Ethnic segregation in Arizona charter schools. *Education Policy Analysis Archives, 7,* No. 1 [On-line]. Available: http://epaa.asu.edu

Cohen, D. C. (1990, Fall). A revolution in one classroom: The case of Mrs. Oublier. *Educational Evaluation and Policy Analysis,* pp. 311-329.

Cohen, R. (1992, August 4). Blame Reagan too. *Washington Post,* p. A19.

Cohn, D'V. (1987, June 21). Test debate: Do higher numbers mean better schools? *Washington Post,* p. A1.

The College Board. (1977). *On further examination: Report of the Advisory Panel on the Scholastic Aptitude Test score decline.* New York: Author.

Cremin, L. (1989). *Public education and its discontents.* New York: Harper and Row.

Crisis in education, Part I: Schoolboys point up U.S. weakness. (1958, March 24). *Life,* pp. 27-35.

Digest of education statistics. (1998). Washington, DC: U.S. Department of Education, Office of Educational Research and Improvement.

Doyle, D. P. (1994). *Where connoisseurs send their children to school: An analysis of 1990 census data to determine where school teachers send their children to school.* Washington, DC: Center for Education Reform.

Doyle, D. P. (1996). Education. In *Issues '96: The candidate's briefing book.* Washington, DC: Heritage Foundation.

Education reform is key to revitalization. (1997, June 9). *Daily Yomiuri,* p. A15.

Eisner, E. (1984, March). Can educational research inform educational practice? *Phi Delta Kappan,* pp. 447-452.

Elley, W. B. (1996). *How in the world do students read?* Hamburg: Grindeldruck GBMH, for the International Association for the Evaluation of Educational Achievement.

Employment outlook, 1996-2006. (1997, November). *Monthly Labor Review* [Entire issue].

Escobar, G. (1999, January 9). Immigrants' ranks tripled in 29 years. *Washington Post,* p. A1.

Featherstone, J. (1967a, August 19). Schools for children. *New Republic,* pp. 17-20.

Featherstone, J. (1967b, September 2). How children learn. *New Republic,* pp. 17-20.

Featherstone, J. (1967c, September 9). Teaching children to think. *New Republic,* pp. 15-19.

Fine, B. (1943, April 4). Ignorance of U.S. history shown by college freshmen. *New York Times,* p. 1.

Finn, C. E., Bierlein, L., & Mann, B. V. (1996). Charter schools in action: A first look. Indianapolis, IN: Hudson Institute.

Finn, J. D., & Achilles, C. M. (1999). Tennessee's class size study: Findings, implications, misconceptions. *Educational Evaluation and Policy Analysis, 21,* 97-110.

Fordham Foundation. (1999). *The teachers we need and how to get more of them.* Washington, DC: Author.

Gelberg, D. (1997). *The "business" of reforming American schools.* Albany: State University of New York Press.

George, P. (1995). *The Japanese secondary school: A closer look.* Reston, VA: National Association of Secondary School Principals.

Gilman, D. (1999). About books. *NASSP Bulletin, 83,* 608, 117-118.

Glaser, R. (1987). A review of the report by a committee of the National Academy of Education. In A. Lamar and J. H. Thomas (Eds.), *The nation's report card: Improving the assessment of student achievement.* Cambridge, MA: National Academy of Education.

Glass, Gene V. (1978, Winter). Standards and criteria. *Journal of Educational Measurement,* pp. 237-261.

Glasser, W. (1990). The quality school. *Phi Delta Kappan, 71,* 424-435.

Greene, P., & Peterson, P. E. (1996, August 14). Choice data rescued from bad science. *Wall Street Journal.*

Grissmer, D. (Ed.). (1999). Class size: Issues and new findings [special issue]. *Educational Evaluation and Policy Analysis, 21,* 93-248.

Hanushek, E. A. (1989). The impact of differential school expenditures on school performance. *Educational Researcher, 18,* 45-51.

Hanushek, E. A. (1999). Some findings from an independent investigation of the Tennessee STAR experiment and from other investigations of class size effects. *Educational Evaluation and Policy Analysis, 21,* 143-164.

Henig, J. (1994). *Rethinking school choice: Limits of the market metaphor.* Princeton, NJ: Princeton University Press.

Herrnstein, R. J., & Murray, C. (1994). *The bell curve.* New York: Free Press.

Hill, P. T., Foster, G. E., & Gendler, T. (1990). *High schools with character.* Santa Monica, CA: RAND Corporation.

Hoffman, B. (1963). *The tyranny of testing.* New York: Greenwood.

Horn, J., & Miron, G. (1999). *Evaluation of the Michigan Public School Initiative, final report.* Kalamazoo: Western Michigan University, Evaluation Center.

Ishizaka, K. (1998). Reforming Japan's schools. *Principal, 77*(3), 24-27.

Johnson, W. B., & Packer, A. H. (1988). *Workforce 2000: Work and workers for the twenty-first century.* Indianapolis, IN: Hudson Institute.

Jones, L. V. (1998). *National tests and education reform: Are they compatible?* Princeton, NJ: Educational Testing Service.

Kelleher, M. (1999, June 1). Dropout rate climbs and schools dump truants. *Catalyst,* p. 1.

Kidder, T. (1989). *Among schoolchildren.* New York: Avon Books.

Killian, C. (1998, February 12-19). Why are boys dumber? *The Georgia Straight,* p. 1.

Kilpatrick, J. J. (1983, May 3). At bottom, Americans just don't give a damn. *Washington Post,* p. A19.

Kolderie, T. (1995). *The charter idea: Update and prospects, Fall 1995, public services redesigns project.* St. Paul, MN: Center for Policy Studies.

Lanford, H., & Wyckoff, J. (1995). Where has the money gone? *Educational Evaluation and Policy Analysis, 17*(20), 195-218.

Lee, J. B. (1984). *Tomorrow's teachers* (Report prepared for U.S. Department of Education, October 25, 1984). ERIC Document Reproduction Service No. ED 263 042.

Lemann, N. (1998). *The big test: The secret history of the American meritocracy.* New York: Farrar, Strauss, Giroux.

Martin, M. O., Mullis, I. V. S., Beaton, A. O., Gonzalez, E. J., Smith, T. A., & Kelly, D. L. (1997). *Science achievement in the primary school years.* Chestnut Hill, MA: Boston College.

Mathews, J. (1999a). *Class struggle: What's wrong (and right) with America's best public high schools.* New York: Times Books.

Mathews, J. (1999b, June 15). The principal's fear of flunking. *Washington Post,* p. A33.

McEwan, P., & Carnoy, M. (1999). *The effectiveness and efficiency of private schools in Chile's voucher system.* Unpublished manuscript, Stanford University School of Education.

Merseth, K. K. (1993). How old is the shepherd? An essay about mathematics education. *Phi Delta Kappan, 75,* 548-552.

Molnar, A. (1996). *Giving kids the business.* Boulder, CO: Westview.

Molnar, A., Smith, P., Zaborik, J., Palmer, A., Halbach, A., & Ehrle, K. (1999). Evaluating the SAGE Program: A pilot program in targeted pupil-teacher reduction in Wisconsin. *Educational Evaluation and Policy Analysis, 21,* 165-178.

Mullis, I. V. S. (1997). *Realistically possible mathematics achievement: Characteristics of the highest performing school systems in the TIMSS.* Paper presented at the annual meeting of the American Educational Research Association, Chicago.

Mullis, I. V. S., Martin, M. O., Beaton, A. E., Gonzalez, E. J., Kelly, D. L., & Smith, T. A. (1997). *Mathematics achievement in the primary school years.* Chestnut Hill, MA: Boston College.

Mullis, I. V. S., Martin, M. O., Beaton, A. E., Gonzalez, E. J., Kelly, D. L., & Smith, T. A. (1998). *Mathematics and science achievement in the final year of secondary school.* Chestnut Hill, MA: Boston College

Murray, C., & Herrnstein, R. (1992). What's really behind the SAT score decline? *The Public Interest, 106,* 26-32.

National Academy of Education. (1987). In L. Alexander & H. T. James (Eds.), *The nation's report card: Improving the assessment of student achievement.* Stanford, CA: Author.

National Commission on Excellence in Education. (1983). *A nation at risk: The imperative for educational reform.* Washington, DC: Author.

National Commission on Teaching and America's Future. (1996). *What matters most.* New York: Author.

National Committee for Responsive Philanthropy. (1997). *Moving a public agenda.* Washington, DC: Author.

Orfield, G., & DeBray, E. (Eds.). (2000). *Hard word for good schools: Facts not fads in Title I.* New York: Center Foundation.

Organization for Economic Cooperation and Development. (1995). *Literacy, economy and society: Results of the First International Adult Literacy Survey.* Paris: Author.

Organization for Economic Cooperation and Development. (1996). *Education at a glance 1996.* Paris: Author.

Organization for Economic Cooperation and Development. (1998). *Education at a glance 1998.* Paris: Author.

O'Sullivan, C. Y., Reese, C. M., & Mazzeo, J. (1997). *NAEP 1996 science report card for the nation and the states.* Washington, DC: U.S. Department of Education, Office of Educational Research and Improvement.

Owen, D. (1985). *None of the above: Behind the myth of scholastic aptitude.* Boston: Houghton Mifflin.

Payne, K., & Biddle, B. (1999, August-September). Poor school funding, child poverty, and mathematics achievement. *Educational Researcher,* pp. 4-13.

Pellegrino, J. W., Jones, L. R., & Mitchell, K. J. (1999). *Grading the nation's report card: Evaluating NAEP and transforming the assessment of educational progress.* Washington, DC: National Academy Press.

Perkinson, H. J. (1991). *The imperfect panacea* (3rd ed.). New York: McGraw-Hill.

Peterson, P. E. (1990). Money and competition in American schools. In W. H. Clune and J. F. Witte (Eds.), *Choice and control in American education*. London: Falmer Press.

Powell, B., & Steelman, L. C. (1996, Spring). Bewitched, bothered, and bewildered: The use and misuse of state SAT and ACT scores. *Harvard Educational Review*, pp. 27-59.

Public Agenda. (1999). *Kids these days '99: What Americans really think about the next generation*. New York: Author.

Rasell, M. E., & Mishel, L. (1990). *Shortchanging education: How U.S. spending on grades K-12 lags behind other industrialized nations*. Washington, DC: Economic Policy Institute.

Ravitch, D. (1996, December 7). Why do Catholic schools succeed? *Forbes*, p. 81.

Ravitch, D. (1999, December 16). What if research really mattered. *Education Week*, p. 33.

Resnick, L. (1989). *Education and learning to think*. Washington, DC: National Research Council.

Rickover, H. G. (1958). *Education and freedom*. New York: E. P. Dutton.

Riley, R. (1998, January). Mathematics equals opportunity. *Community Update* [U.S. Department of Education newsletter].

Rofes, E. (1998). *How are school districts responding to charter laws and charter schools?* Berkeley: University of California, Policy Analysis for California Education.

Rotberg, I. (1998, May 15). Interpretation of international score comparisons. *Science*, pp. 1030-1031.

Rothstein, R. (1997). *What do we know about declining (or rising) student achievement*. Arlington, VA: Educational Research Service.

Rothstein, R. (1999). *A composite accountability system for the Los Angeles Unified School District: Part 1. Principles of school accountability* [On-line]. Available: www.epn.org/rothstein/Lausd/LAUSDindex1.html

Rothstein, R., Carnoy, M., & Benveniste, L. (1999). *What can public schools learn from the private, non-profit education sector*. Washington, DC: Economic Policy Institute.

Rothstein, R., & Miles, K. H. (1995). *Where's the money gone: Changes in the level and composition of education spending*. Washington, DC: Economic Policy Institute.

Rouse, C. E. (1998, March). Schools and student achievement: More evidence from the Milwaukee Parental Choice Program. *Federal Reserve Bank of New York Economic Policy Review*. (Available by subscription from the Federal Reserve Bank)

Salmon, P. B. (1983). [Statement accompanying the reproduction of *A nation at risk* by the American Association of School Administrators.] (Available from American Association of School Administrators, 1801 North Moore Street, Arlington, VA 22209)

Sanchez, R. (1998, February 25). U.S. high school seniors rank near bottom. *Washington Post,* p. A1.

Sanders, W. L. (1998). Value-added assessment. *The School Administrator, 55*(11), 24-29.

Sanders, W. L., & Rivers, J. C. (1996). *Cumulative and residual effects of teachers on future student academic achievement.* Knoxville: University of Tennessee Value-Added Research and Assessment Center.

Schmidt, W. H., McKnight, C. C., Valverde, G. A., Houang, R. T., & Wiley, D. E. (1996). *Many visions, many aims: A cross-national investigation of curricular intentions in school mathematics.* Boston: Kluwer Academic.

Schmidt, W. H., Raizen, S. A., Britton, E. D., Bianchi, L. J., & Wolfe, R. G. (1996). *Many visions, many aims: A cross-national investigation of curricular intentions in school science.* Boston: Kluwer Academic.

Schooland, K. (1989). *Shogun's ghosts: The dark side of Japanese education.* New York: Bergin & Garvey.

Shanker, A., & Rosenberg, B. (1992). Do private schools outperform public schools? In P. Cookson, Jr. (Ed.), *The choice controversy.* Newbury Park, CA: Corwin.

Shaver, J. P. (1985a). Chance and nonsense: A conversation about interpreting tests of statistical significance, part I. *Phi Delta Kappan, 67,* 57-60.

Shaver, J. P. (1985b). Chance and nonsense: A conversation about interpreting tests of statistical significance, part II. *Phi Delta Kappan, 67,* 138-141.

Shepard, L. A., & Smith, M. L. (1989). *Flunking grades: Research and policies on retention.* New York: Falmer.

Shokraii, N. (1997). *Why Catholic schools mean success for America's inner-city children* (Backgrounder No. 1128, June 30). Washington, DC: Heritage Foundation.

Silberman, C. (1970). *Crisis in the classroom.* New York: Random House.

Starch, D., & Elliott, E. (1912, September). Reliability of grading high school work in English. *The School Review,* pp. 442-459.

Stecher, B. M., & Bohrnstedt, G. W. (1999). *Class size reduction in California: Early evaluation findings.* Los Angeles: Class Size Reduction Research Consortium.

Stevenson, H., & Stigler, J. (1992). *The learning gap.* New York: Summit Books.

Teacher knows best. (1993, October 25). *Wall Street Journal,* p. 20.

Thernstrom, S. (1998). Introduction to volume 9. *The Concord Review,* Fall.

Toch, T. (1998, April 12). Education bazaar. *U.S. News and World Report,* pp. 35-46.

Todd, C., Mitchel, K., Matthews, P., Riordan, N., & Nowicki, D. (1998, August 24-28). Guinea kids: Arizona's charter school experiment. *Arizona Tribune,* p. 1. [Daily front page feature]

University of Tennessee Value-Added Research and Assessment Center. (1997). *Graphical summary of educational findings from the Tennessee value-added assessment system.* Knoxville: Author.

Van Wolferen, K. (1989). *The enigma of Japanese power.* New York: Knopf.

Viadero, D. (1998, March 4). U.S. seniors near bottom in world test. *Education Week,* p. 1.

Wainer, H. (1993). Does spending money on education help? *Educational Researcher, 23*(10), 22-24.

Wainer, H., & Steinberg, L. (1992, Fall). Sex differences in performance on the mathmatic section of the Scholastic Aptitude Test: A bidirectional validity study. *Harvard Educational Review,* pp. 323-326.

Wells, A. S. (1998). *Beyond the rhetoric of charter school reform: A study of ten California school districts.* Los Angeles: University of California at Los Angeles Graduate School of Education and Information Studies.

Will, G. F. (1993a, September 12). Meaningless money factor. *Washington Post,* p. C7.

Will, G. F. (1993b, August 26). Taking back education. *Washington Post,* p. A27.

Will, G. F. (1993c, March 7). When the state fails its citizens. *Washington Post,* p. C7.

Wilson, S. (1958, March 24). It's time to close our circus. *Life,* pp. 31-32.

Worthen, B., & Spanel, V. (1991). Putting the standardized testing debate in perspective. *Educational Leadership, 49,* 67-71.

Wurtzel, A. (1993, December 7). Getting from school to work. *Washington Post,* p. A25.

Yankelovich, D. (1998). Public opinion and the youth of America. In S. Halperin (Ed.), *The forgotten half revisited.* Washington, DC: American Youth Policy Forum.

CORWIN
PRESS

The Corwin Press logo—a raven striding across an open book—represents the happy union of courage and learning. We are a professional-level publisher of books and journals for K-12 educators, and we are committed to creating and providing resources that embody these qualities. Corwin's motto is "Success for All Learners."